Things Fall Apart

with Connections

Things Fall Apart

Chinua Achebe

with
Connections

HOLT, RINEHART AND WINSTON
Harcourt Brace & Company

Austin • New York • Orlando • Atlanta • San Francisco
Boston • Dallas • Toronto • London

For permission to reprint copyrighted material, grateful acknowledgment is made to the following sources:

Heinemann Educational Publishers: *Things Fall Apart* by Chinua Achebe. Copyright © 1958 by Chinua Achebe.

O. O. Enekwe on behalf of the author: From "The Garden of Evil" by William Saidi from Nigerian literary periodical *Okike.* Copyright © 1976 by Okike. **Uche Okeke:** From "Old Sayings" and "Okuku's Chickens" from *Tales of Land of Death: Igbo Folktales,* told and illustrated by Uche Okeke. Copyright © 1971 by Doubleday & Company; copyright © 1992 by Uche Okeke. **Patrick H. Samway:** "An Interview with Chinua Achebe" by Patrick H. Samway from *America,* vol. 164, no. 24, June 22–29, 1991. Copyright © 1991 by Patrick H. Samway. **Sonia Sanchez:** From "Nigerian Bard Tells His Own Story" by Sonia Sanchez from *Emerge,* vol. 6, no. 5, March 1995. Copyright © 1995 by Sonia Sanchez. **Simon & Schuster, Inc.:** "The Second Coming" from *The Poems of W. B. Yeats: A New Edition,* edited by Richard J. Finneran. Copyright © 1924 by Macmillan Publishing Company; copyright renewed 1952 by Bertha Georgie Yeats. **Vintage Books, a division of Random House, Inc.:** Excerpt (retitled "The Jungle Commission") from *Facing Mount Kenya: The Tribal Life of the Gikuyu* by Jomo Kenyatta. Copyright 1938 by Secker and Warburg, Ltd.; copyright renewed © 1962 by Vintage Books, a division of Random House, Inc.

Cover: Earl Keleny

ISBN 0-03-055438-1

18 19 20 21   043   09 08

Contents

PART ONE

One

OKONKWO was well known throughout the nine villages and even beyond. His fame rested on solid personal achievements. As a young man of eighteen he
had brought honor to his village by throwing Amalinze the Cat. Amalinze was the great wrestler who for
seven years was unbeaten, from Umuofia to Mbaino.
He was called the Cat because his back would never
touch the earth. It was this man that Okonkwo threw
in a fight which the old men agreed was one of the
fiercest since the founder of their town engaged a
spirit of the wild for seven days and seven nights.

The drums beat and the flutes sang and the spectators held their breath. Amalinze was a wily crafts-
man, but Okonkwo was as slippery as a fish in water.
Every nerve and every muscle stood out on their arms,
on their backs and their thighs, and one almost heard
them stretching to breaking point. In the end Okonkwo threw the Cat.

That was many years ago, twenty years or more, and
during this time Okonkwo's fame had grown like a
bush-fire in the harmattan. He was tall and huge, and
his bushy eyebrows and wide nose gave him a very
severe look. He breathed heavily, and it was said that,
when he slept, his wives and children in their houses
could hear him breathe. When he walked, his heels
hardly touched the ground and he seemed to walk on
springs, as if he was going to pounce on somebody.
And he did pounce on people quite often. He had a
slight stammer and whenever he was angry and could

1

not get his words out quickly enough, he would use his fists. He had no patience with unsuccessful men. He had had no patience with his father.

Unoka, for that was his father's name, had died ten years ago. In his day he was lazy and improvident and was quite incapable of thinking about tomorrow. If any money came his way, and it seldom did, he immediately bought gourds of palm-wine, called round his neighbors and made merry. He always said that whenever he saw a dead man's mouth he saw the folly of not eating what one had in one's lifetime. Unoka was, of course, a debtor, and he owed every neighbor some money, from a few cowries to quite substantial amounts.

He was tall but very thin and had a slight stoop. He wore a haggard and mournful look except when he was drinking or playing on his flute. He was very good on his flute, and his happiest moments were the two or three moons after the harvest when the village musicians brought down their instruments, hung above the fireplace. Unoka would play with them, his face beaming with blessedness and peace. Sometimes another village would ask Unoka's band and their dancing *egwugwu* to come and stay with them and teach them their tunes. They would go to such hosts for as long as three or four markets, making music and feasting. Unoka loved the good fare and the good fellowship, and he loved this season of the year, when the rains had stopped and the sun rose every morning with dazzling beauty. And it was not too hot either, because the cold and dry harmattan wind was blowing down from the north. Some years the harmattan was very severe and a dense haze hung on the atmosphere. Old men and children would then sit round log fires, warming their bodies. Unoka loved it all, and he loved the first kites that returned with the dry

2

season, and the children who sang songs of welcome to them. He would remember his own childhood, how he had often wandered around looking for a kite sailing leisurely against the blue sky. As soon as he found one he would sing with his whole being, welcoming it back from its long, long journey, and asking it if it had brought home any lengths of cloth.

That was years ago, when he was young. Unoka, the grown-up, was a failure. He was poor and his wife and children had barely enough to eat. People laughed at him because he was a loafer, and they swore never to lend him any more money because he never paid back. But Unoka was such a man that he always succeeded in borrowing more, and piling up his debts.

One day a neighbor called Okoye came in to see him. He was reclining on a mud bed in his hut playing on the flute. He immediately rose and shook hands with Okoye, who then unrolled the goatskin which he carried under his arm, and sat down. Unoka went into an inner room and soon returned with a small wooden disc containing a kola nut, some alligator pepper and a lump of white chalk.

'I have kola,' he announced when he sat down, and passed the disc over to his guest.

'Thank you. He who brings kola brings life. But I think you ought to break it,' replied Okoye, passing back the disc.

'No, it is for you, I think,' and they argued like this for a few moments before Unoka accepted the honor of breaking the kola. Okoye, meanwhile, took the lump of chalk, drew some lines on the floor, and then painted his big toe.

As he broke the kola, Unoka prayed to their ancestors for life and health, and for protection against their enemies. When they had eaten they talked about many things: about the heavy rains which were drowning the yams, about the next ancestral feast and about the impending war with the village of Mbaino. Unoka was never happy when it came to wars. He was in fact a coward and could not bear the sight of blood. And so he changed the subject and talked about music, and his face beamed. He could hear in his mind's ear the blood-stirring and intricate rhythms of the *ekwe* and the *udu* and the *ogene*, and he could hear his own flute weaving in and out of them, decorating them with a colorful and plaintive tune. The total effect was gay and brisk, but if one picked out the flute as it went up and down and then broke up into short snatches, one saw that there was sorrow and grief there.

Okoye was also a musician. He played on the *ogene*. But he was not a failure like Unoka. He had a large barn full of yams and he had three wives. And now he was going to take the Idemili title, the third highest in the land. It was a very expensive ceremony and he was gathering all his resources together. That was in fact the reason why he had come to see Unoka. He cleared his throat and began:

'Thank you for the kola. You may have heard of the title I intend to take shortly.'

Having spoken plainly so far, Okoye said the next half a dozen sentences in proverbs. Among the Ibo the art of conversation is regarded very highly, and proverbs are the palm-oil with which words are eaten. Okoye was a great talker and he spoke for a long time, skirting round the subject and then hitting it finally. In short, he was asking Unoka to return the two hundred cowries he had borrowed from him more than two years before. As soon as Unoka understood what his friend was driving at, he burst out laughing. He laughed loud and long and his voice rang out clear as the *ogene*, and tears stood in his eyes. His visitor was amazed, and sat speechless. At the end, Unoka was able to give an answer between fresh outbursts of mirth.

'Look at that wall,' he said, pointing at the far wall of his hut, which was rubbed with red earth so that it shone. 'Look at those lines of chalk;' and Okoye saw groups of short perpendicular lines drawn in chalk. There were five groups, and the smallest group had ten lines. Unoka had a sense of the dramatic and so he allowed a pause, in which he took a pinch of snuff and sneezed noisily, and then he continued: 'Each group there represents a debt to someone, and each stroke is one hundred cowries. You see, I owe that man a thousand cowries. But he has not come to wake me up in the morning for it. I shall pay you, but not today. Our elders say that the sun will shine on those who stand before it shines on those who kneel under them. I shall pay my big debts first.' And he took another pinch of snuff, as if that was paying the big debts first. Okoye rolled his goatskin and departed.

When Unoka died he had taken no title at all and he was heavily in debt. Any wonder then that his son Okonkwo was ashamed of him? Fortunately, among these people a man was judged according to his worth and not according to the worth of his father. Okonkwo was clearly cut out for great things. He was still young but he had won fame as the greatest wrestler in the nine villages. He was a wealthy farmer and had two barns full of yams, and had just married his third wife. To crown it all he had taken two titles and had shown incredible prowess in two inter-tribal wars. And so although Okonkwo was still young, he was already one of the greatest men of his time. Age was respected among his people, but achievement was revered. As the elders said, if a child washed his hands he could eat with kings. Okonkwo had clearly washed his hands

CHINUA ACHEBE

and so he ate with kings and elders. And that was how he came to look after the doomed lad who was sacrificed to the village of Umuofia by their neighbors to avoid war and bloodshed. The ill-fated lad was called Ikemefuna.

6

Two

OKONKWO had just blown out the palm-oil lamp and stretched himself on his bamboo bed when he heard the *ogene* of the town crier piercing the still night air. *Gome, gome, gome, gome,* boomed the hollow metal. Then the crier gave his message, and at the end of it beat his instrument again. And this was the message. Every man of Umuofia was asked to gather at the market place tomorrow morning. Okonkwo wondered what was amiss, for he knew certainly that something was amiss. He had discerned a clear overtone of tragedy in the crier's voice, and even now he could still hear it as it grew dimmer and dimmer in the distance.

The night was very quiet. It was always quiet except on moonlight nights. Darkness held a vague terror for these people, even the bravest among them. Children were warned not to whistle at night for fear of evil spirits. Dangerous animals became even more sinister and uncanny in the dark. A snake was never called by its name at night, because it would hear. It was called a string. And so on this particular night as the crier's voice was gradually swallowed up in the distance, silence returned to the world, a vibrant silence made more intense by the universal trill of a million million forest insects.

On a moonlight night it would be different. The happy voices of children playing in open fields would then be heard. And perhaps those not so young would be playing in pairs in less open places, and old men and women would remember their youth. As the Ibo say: 'When the moon is shining the cripple becomes hungry for a walk.'

But this particular night was dark and silent. And in all the nine villages of Umuofia a town crier with his *ogene* asked every man to be present tomorrow morning. Okonkwo on his bamboo bed tried to figure out the nature of the emergency – war with a neighboring clan? That seemed the most likely reason, and he was not afraid of war. He was a man of action, a man of war. Unlike his father he could stand the look of blood. In Umuofia's latest war he was the first to bring home a human head. That was his fifth head; and he was not an old man yet. On great occasions such as the funeral of a village celebrity he drank his palm-wine from his first human head.

In the morning the market place was full. There must have been about ten thousand men there, all talking in low voices. At last Ogbuefi Ezeugo stood up in the midst of them and bellowed four times, '*Umuofia kwenu,*' and on each occasion he faced a different direction and seemed to push the air with a clenched fist. And ten thousand men answered '*Yaa!*' each time. Then there was perfect silence. Ogbuefi Ezeugo was a powerful orator and was always chosen to speak on such occasions. He moved his hand over his white head and stroked his white beard. He then adjusted his cloth, which was passed under his right arm-pit and tied above his left shoulder.

'*Umuofia kwenu,*' he bellowed a fifth time, and the crowd yelled in answer. And then suddenly like one possessed he shot out his left hand and pointed in the direction of Mbaino, and said through gleaming white teeth firmly clenched: 'Those sons of wild animals have dared to murder a daughter of Umuofia.' He threw his head down and gnashed his teeth, and allowed a murmur of suppressed anger to sweep the crowd. When he began again, the anger on his face was gone and in its place a sort of smile hovered, more terrible and more sinister than the anger. And in a clear unemotional voice he told Umuofia how their daughter had gone to market at Mbaino and had been killed. That woman, said Ezeugo, was the wife of Ogbuefi Udo, and he pointed to a man who sat near him with a bowed head. The crowd then shouted with anger and thirst for blood.

Many others spoke, and at the end it was decided to follow the normal course of action. An ultimatum was immediately dispatched to Mbaino asking them to choose between war on the one hand, and on the other the offer of a young man and a virgin as compensation.

Umuofia was feared by all its neighbors. It was powerful in war and in magic, and its priests and medicine men were feared in all the surrounding country. Its most potent war-medicine was as old as the clan itself. Nobody knew how old. But on one point there was general agreement – the active principle in that medicine had been an old woman with one leg. In fact, the medicine itself was called *agadi-nwayi*, or old woman. It had its shrine in the center of Umuofia, in a cleared spot. And if anybody was so foolhardy as to pass by the shrine after dusk he was sure to see the old woman hopping about.

And so the neighboring clans who naturally knew of these things feared Umuofia, and would not go to war against it without first trying a peaceful settlement. And in fairness to Umuofia it should be recorded that it never went to war unless its case was clear and just and was accepted as such by its Oracle – the Oracle of the Hills and the Caves. And there were indeed occasions when the Oracle had forbidden Umuofia to wage a war. If the clan had disobeyed the Oracle they would surely have been beaten, because their dreaded *agadi-nwayi* would never fight what the Ibo call *a fight of blame.*

But the war that now threatened was a just war. Even the enemy clan knew that. And so when Okonkwo of Umuofia arrived at Mbaino as the proud and imperious emissary of war, he was treated with great honor and respect, and two days later he returned home with a lad of fifteen and a young virgin. The lad's name was Ikemefuna, whose sad story is still told in Umuofia unto this day.

The elders, or *ndichie*, met to hear a report of Okonkwo's mission. At the end they decided, as everybody knew they would, that the girl should go to Ogbuefi Udo to replace his murdered wife. As for the boy, he belonged to the clan as a whole, and there was no hurry to decide his fate. Okonkwo was, therefore, asked on behalf of the clan to look after him in the interim. And so for three years Ikemefuna lived in Okonkwo's household.

Okonkwo ruled his household with a heavy hand. His wives, especially the youngest, lived in perpetual fear of his fiery temper, and so did his little children. Perhaps down in his heart Okonkwo was not a cruel man. But his whole life was dominated by fear, the fear of failure and of weakness. It was deeper and more intimate than the fear of evil and capricious gods and of magic, the fear of the forest, and of the forces of nature, malevolent, red in tooth and claw. Okonkwo's fear was greater than these. It was not external but lay deep within himself. It was the fear of himself, lest he should be found to resemble his father. Even as a little boy he had resented his father's failure and weakness, and even now he still remembered how he had suffered when a playmate had told him that his father was *agbala*. That was how Okonkwo first came to know that *agbala* was not only another name for a woman, it could also mean a man who had taken no title. And so Okonkwo was ruled by one passion – to hate everything that his father Unoka had loved. One of those things was gentleness and another was idleness.

During the planting season Okonkwo worked daily on his farms from cock-crow until the chickens went to roost. He was a very strong man and rarely felt fatigue. But his wives and young children were not as strong, and so they suffered. But they dared not complain openly. Okonkwo's first son, Nwoye, was then twelve years old but was already causing his father great anxiety for his incipient laziness. At any rate, that was how it looked to his father, and he sought to correct him by constant nagging and beating. And so Nwoye was developing into a sad-faced youth.

Okonkwo's prosperity was visible in his household. He had a large compound enclosed by a thick wall of red earth. His own hut, or *obi*, stood immediately behind the only gate in the red walls. Each of his three wives had her own hut, which together formed a half moon behind the *obi*. The barn was built against one end of the red walls, and long stacks of yam stood out prosperously in it. At the opposite end of the compound was a shed for the goats, and each wife built a small attachment to her hut for the hens. Near the barn was a small house, the 'medicine house' or shrine where Okonkwo kept the wooden symbols of his personal god and of his ancestral spirits. He worshipped them with sacrifices of kola nut, food and palm-wine, and offered prayers to them on behalf of himself, his three wives and eight children.

*

So when the daughter of Umuofia was killed in Mbaino, Ikemefuna came into Okonkwo's household. When Okonkwo brought him home that day he called his most senior wife and handed him over to her.

'He belongs to the clan,' he told her. 'So look after him.'

'Is he staying long with us?' she asked.

'Do what you are told, woman,' Okonkwo thundered, and stammered. 'When did you become one of the *ndichie* of Umuofia?'

And so Nwoye's mother took Ikemefuna to her hut and asked no more questions.

As for the boy himself, he was terribly afraid. He could not understand what was happening to him or what he had done. How could he know that his father had taken a hand in killing a daughter of Umuofia? All he knew was that a few men had arrived at their house, conversing with his father in low tones, and at the end he had been taken out and handed over to a stranger. His mother had wept bitterly, but he had been too surprised to weep. And so the stranger had brought him, and a girl, a long, long way from home, through lonely forest paths. He did not know who the girl was, and he never saw her again.

Three

OKONKWO did not have the start in life which many young men usually had. He did not inherit a barn from his father. There was no barn to inherit. The story was told in Umuofia of how his father, Unoka, had gone to consult the Oracle of the Hills and the Caves to find out why he always had a miserable harvest.

The Oracle was called Agbala, and people came from far and near to consult it. They came when misfortune dogged their steps or when they had a dispute with their neighbors. They came to discover what the future held for them or to consult the spirits of their departed fathers.

The way into the shrine was a round hole at the side of a hill, just a little bigger than the round opening into a henhouse. Worshippers and those who came to seek knowledge from the god crawled on their belly through the hole and found themselves in a dark, endless space in the presence of Agbala. No one had ever beheld Agbala, except his priestess. But no one who had ever crawled into his awful shrine had come out without the fear of his power. His priestess stood by the sacred fire which she built in the heart of the cave and proclaimed the will of the god. The fire did not burn with a flame. The glowing logs only served to light up vaguely the dark figure of the priestess.

Sometimes a man came to consult the spirit of his dead father or relative. It was said that when such a spirit appeared, the man saw it vaguely in the darkness, but never heard its voice. Some people even said that they had heard the spirits flying and flapping their wings against the roof of the cave.

Many years ago when Okonkwo was still a boy his father, Unoka, had gone to consult Agbala. The priestess in those days was a woman called Chika. She was full of the power of her god, and she was greatly feared. Unoka stood before her and began his story.

'Every year,' he said sadly, 'before I put any crop in the earth, I sacrifice a cock to Ani, the owner of all land. It is the law of our fathers. I also kill a cock at the shrine of Ifejioku, the god of yams. I clear the bush and set fire to it when it is dry. I sow the yams when the first rain has fallen, and stake them when the young tendrils appear. I weed –'

'Hold your peace!' screamed the priestess, her voice terrible as it echoed through the dark void. 'You have offended neither the gods nor your fathers. And when a man is at peace with his gods and his ancestors, his harvest will be good or bad according to the strength of his arm. You, Unoka, are known in all the clan for the weakness of your machete and your hoe. When your neighbors go out with their ax to cut down virgin forests, you sow your yams on exhausted farms that take no labor to clear. They cross seven rivers to make their farms; you stay at home and offer sacrifices to a reluctant soil. Go home and work like a man.'

Unoka was an ill-fated man. He had a bad *chi* or personal god, and evil fortune followed him to the grave, or rather to his death, for he had no grave. He died of the swelling which was an abomination to the earth goddess. When a man was afflicted with swelling in the stomach and the limbs he was not allowed to die in the house. He was carried to the Evil Forest and left there to die. There was the story of a very stubborn man who staggered back to his house and had

to be carried again to the forest and tied to a tree.
The sickness was an abomination to the earth, and so
the victim could not be buried in her bowels. He died
and rotted away above the earth, and was not given
the first or the second burial. Such was Unoka's fate.
When they carried him away, he took with him his
flute.

With a father like Unoka, Okonkwo did not have
the start in life which many young men had. He
neither inherited a barn nor a title, nor even a young
wife. But in spite of these disadvantages, he had begun
even in his father's lifetime to lay the foundations of
a prosperous future. It was slow and painful. But he
threw himself into it like one possessed. And indeed
he was possessed by the fear of his father's contempt-
ible life and shameful death.

There was a wealthy man in Okonkwo's village who
had three huge barns, nine wives and thirty children.
His name was Nwakibie and he had taken the highest
but one title which a man could take in the clan. It was
for this man that Okonkwo worked to earn his first
seed yams.

He took a pot of palm-wine and a cock to Nwakibie.
Two elderly neighbors were sent for, and Nwakibie's
two grown-up sons were also present in his *obi.* He
presented a kola nut and an alligator pepper, which
were passed round for all to see and then returned to
him. He broke the nut saying: 'We shall all live. We
pray for life, children, a good harvest and happiness.
You will have what is good for you and I will have what
is good for me. Let the kite perch and let the eagle
perch too. If one says no to the other, let his wing
break.'

After the kola nut had been eaten Okonkwo

brought his palm-wine from the corner of the hut where it had been placed and stood it in the center of the group. He addressed Nwakibie, calling him 'Our father.'

'*Nna ayi*,' he said. 'I have brought you this little kola. As our people say, a man who pays respect to the great paves the way for his own greatness. I have come to pay you my respects and also to ask a favor. But let us drink the wine first.'

Everybody thanked Okonkwo and the neighbors brought out their drinking horns from the goatskin bags they carried. Nwakibie brought down his own horn, which was fastened to the rafters. The younger of his sons, who was also the youngest man in the group, moved to the center, raised the pot on his left knee and began to pour out the wine. The first cup went to Okonkwo, who must taste his wine before anyone else. Then the group drank, beginning with the eldest man. When everyone had drunk two or three horns, Nwakibie sent for his wives. Some of them were not at home and only four came in.

'Is Anasi not in?' he asked them. They said she was coming. Anasi was the first wife and the others could not drink before her, and so they stood waiting.

Anasi was a middle-aged woman, tall and strongly built. There was authority in her bearing and she looked every inch the ruler of the womenfolk in a large and prosperous family. She wore the anklet of her husband's titles, which the first wife alone could wear.

She walked up to her husband and accepted the horn from him. She then went down on one knee, drank a little and handed back the horn. She rose, called him by his name and went back to her hut. The other wives drank in the same way, in their proper order, and went away.

The men then continued their drinking and talking. Ogbuefi Idigo was talking about the palm-wine tapper, Obiako, who suddenly gave up his trade.

'There must be something behind it,' he said, wiping the foam of wine from his mustache with the back of his left hand. 'There must be a reason for it. A toad does not run in the daytime for nothing.'

'Some people say the Oracle warned him that he would fall off a palm tree and kill himself,' said Akukalia.

'Obiako has always been a strange one,' said Nwakibie. 'I have heard that many years ago, when his father had not been dead very long, he had gone to consult the Oracle. The Oracle said to him, "Your dead father wants you to sacrifice a goat to him." Do you know what he told the Oracle? He said, "Ask my dead father if he ever had a fowl when he was alive."' Everybody laughed heartily except Okonkwo, who laughed uneasily because, as the saying goes, an old woman is always uneasy when dry bones are mentioned in a proverb. Okonkwo remembered his own father.

At last the young man who was pouring out the wine held up half a horn of the thick, white dregs and said, 'What we are eating is finished.' 'We have seen it,' the others replied. 'Who will drink the dregs?' he asked. 'Whoever has a job in hand,' said Idigo, looking at Nwakibie's elder son Igwelo with a malicious twinkle in his eye.

Everybody agreed that Igwelo should drink the dregs. He accepted the half-full horn from his brother and drank it. As Idigo had said, Igwelo had a job in hand because he had married his first wife a month or two before. The thick dregs of palm-wine were supposed to be good for men who were going in to their wives.

17

After the wine had been drunk Okonkwo laid his difficulties before Nwakibie.

'I have come to you for help,' he said. 'Perhaps you can already guess what it is. I have cleared a farm but have no yams to sow. I know what it is to ask a man to trust another with his yams, especially these days when young men are afraid of hard work. I am not afraid of work. The lizard that jumped from the high iroko tree to the ground said he would praise himself if no one else did. I began to fend for myself at an age when most people still suck at their mothers' breasts. If you give me some yam seeds I shall not fail you.'

Nwakibie cleared his throat. 'It pleases me to see a young man like you these days when our youth has gone so soft. Many young men have come to me to ask for yams but I have refused because I knew they would just dump them in the earth and leave them to be choked by weeds. When I say no to them they think I am hard-hearted. But it is not so. Eneke the bird says that since men have learned to shoot without missing, he has learned to fly without perching. I have learned to be stingy with my yams. But I can trust you. I know it as I look at you. As our fathers said, you can tell a ripe corn by its look. I shall give you twice four hundred yams. Go ahead and prepare your farm.'

Okonkwo thanked him again and again and went home feeling happy. He knew that Nwakibie would not refuse him, but he had not expected he would be so generous. He had not hoped to get more than four hundred seeds. He would now have to make a bigger farm. He hoped to get another four hundred yams from one of his father's friends at Isiuzo.

Share-cropping was a very slow way of building up a barn of one's own. After all the toil one only got a third of the harvest. But for a young man whose father had no yams, there was no other way. And what made it worse in Okonkwo's case was that he had to support his mother and two sisters from his meagre harvest. And supporting his mother also meant supporting his father. She could not be expected to cook and eat while her husband starved. And so at a very early age when he was striving desperately to build a barn through share-cropping Okonkwo was also fending for his father's house. It was like pouring grains of corn into a bag full of holes. His mother and sisters worked hard enough, but they grew women's crops, like coco-yams, beans and cassava. Yam, the king of crops, was a man's crop.

The year that Okonkwo took eight hundred seed-yams from Nwakibie was the worst year in living memory. Nothing happened at its proper time; it was either too early or too late. It seemed as if the world had gone mad. The first rains were late, and, when they came, lasted only a brief moment. The blazing sun returned, more fierce than it had ever been known, and scorched all the green that had appeared with the rains. The earth burned like hot coals and roasted all the yams that had been sown. Like all good farmers, Okonkwo had begun to sow with the first rains. He had sown four hundred seeds when the rains dried up and the heat returned. He watched the sky all day for signs of rain clouds and lay awake all night. In the morning he went back to his farm and saw the withering tendrils. He had tried to protect them from the smoldering earth by making rings of thick sisal leaves around them. But by the end of the day the sisal rings were burned dry and gray. He changed them every day, and prayed that the rain might fall in the night. But the drought continued for eight market weeks and the yams were killed.

CHINUA ACHEBE

Some farmers had not planted their yams yet. They were the lazy easy-going ones who always put off clearing their farms as long as they could. This year they were the wise ones. They sympathized with their neighbors with much shaking of the head, but inwardly they were happy for what they took to be their own foresight.

Okonkwo planted what was left of his seed-yams when the rains finally returned. He had one consolation. The yams he had sown before the drought were his own, the harvest of the previous year. He still had the eight hundred from Nwakibie and the four hundred from his father's friend. So he would make a fresh start.

But the year had gone mad. Rain fell as it had never fallen before. For days and nights together it poured down in violent torrents, and washed away the yam heaps. Trees were uprooted and deep gorges appeared everywhere. Then the rain became less violent. But it went from day to day without a pause. The spell of sunshine which always came in the middle of the wet season did not appear. The yams put on luxuriant green leaves, but every farmer knew that without sunshine the tubers would not grow.

That year the harvest was sad, like a funeral, and many farmers wept as they dug up the miserable and rotting yams. One man tied his cloth to a tree branch and hanged himself.

Okonkwo remembered that tragic year with a cold shiver throughout the rest of his life. It always surprised him when he thought of it later that he did not sink under the load of despair. He knew that he was a fierce fighter, but that year had been enough to break the heart of a lion.

'Since I survived that year,' he always said, 'I shall survive anything.' He put it down to his inflexible will.

His father, Unoka, who was then an ailing man, had said to him during that terrible harvest month: 'Do not despair. I know you will not despair. You have a manly and a proud heart. A proud heart can survive a general failure because such a failure does not prick its pride. It is more difficult and more bitter when a man fails *alone*.'

Unoka was like that in his last days. His love of talk had grown with age and sickness. It tried Okonkwo's patience beyond words.

Four

'LOOKING at a king's mouth,' said an old man, 'one would think he never sucked at his mother's breast.' He was talking about Okonkwo, who had risen so suddenly from great poverty and misfortune to be one of the lords of the clan. The old man bore no ill will towards Okonkwo. Indeed he respected him for his industry and success. But he was struck, as most people were, by Okonkwo's brusqueness in dealing with less successful men. Only a week ago a man had contradicted him at a kindred meeting which they held to discuss the next ancestral feast. Without looking at the man Okonkwo had said: 'This meeting is for men.' The man who had contradicted him had no titles. That was why he had called him a woman. Okonkwo knew how to kill a man's spirit.

Everybody at the kindred meeting took sides with Osugo when Okonkwo called him a woman. The oldest man present said sternly that those whose palm-kernels were cracked for them by a benevolent spirit should not forget to be humble. Okonkwo said he was sorry for what he had said, and the meeting continued.

But it was really not true that Okonkwo's palm-kernels had been cracked for him by a benevolent spirit. He had cracked them himself. Anyone who knew his grim struggle against poverty and misfortune could not say he had been lucky. If ever a man deserved his success, that man was Okonkwo. At an early age he had achieved fame as the greatest wrestler in all the land. That was not luck. At the most one could say that his *chi* or personal god was good. But the Ibo people have a proverb that when a man says yes his *chi* says yes also. Okonkwo said yes very strongly; so his *chi* agreed. And not only his *chi* but his clan too, because it judged a man by the work of his hands. That was why Okonkwo had been chosen by the nine villages to carry a message of war to their enemies unless they agreed to give up a young man and a virgin to atone for the murder of Udo's wife. And such was the deep fear that their enemies had for Umuofia that they treated Okonkwo like a king and brought him a virgin who was given to Udo as wife, and the lad Ikemefuna.

The elders of the clan had decided that Ikemefuna should be in Okonkwo's care for a while. But no one thought it would be as long as three years. They seemed to forget all about him as soon as they had taken the decision.

At first Ikemefuna was very much afraid. Once or twice he tried to run away, but he did not know where to begin. He thought of his mother and his three-year-old sister and wept bitterly. Nwoye's mother was very kind to him and treated him as one of her own children. But all he said was: 'When shall I go home?' When Okonkwo heard that he would not eat any food he came into the hut with a big stick in his hand and stood over him while he swallowed his yams, trembling. A few moments later he went behind the hut and began to vomit painfully. Nwoye's mother went to him and placed her hands on his chest and on his back. He was ill for three market weeks, and when he recovered he seemed to have overcome his great fear and sadness.

He was by nature a very lively boy and he gradually became popular in Okonkwo's household, especially with the children. Okonkwo's son, Nwoye, who was two years younger, became quite inseparable from him because he seemed to know everything. He could fashion out flutes from bamboo stems and even from the elephant grass. He knew the names of all the birds and could set clever traps for the little bush rodents. And he knew which trees made the strongest bows.

Even Okonkwo himself became very fond of the boy – inwardly of course. Okonkwo never showed any emotion openly, unless it be the emotion of anger. To show affection was a sign of weakness; the only thing worth demonstrating was strength. He therefore treated Ikemefuna as he treated everybody else – with a heavy hand. But there was no doubt that he liked the boy. Sometimes when he went to big village meetings or communal ancestral feasts he allowed Ikemefuna to accompany him, like a son, carrying his stool and his goatskin bag. And, indeed, Ikemefuna called him father.

Ikemefuna came to Umuofia at the end of the carefree season between harvest and planting. In fact he recovered from his illness only a few days before the Week of Peace began. And that was also the year Okonkwo broke the peace, and was punished, as was the custom, by Ezeani, the priest of the earth goddess.

Okonkwo was provoked to justifiable anger by his youngest wife, who went to plait her hair at her friend's house and did not return early enough to cook the afternoon meal. Okonkwo did not know at first that she was not at home. After waiting in vain for her dish he went to her hut to see what she was doing. There was nobody in the hut and the fireplace was cold.

'Where is Ojiugo?' he asked his second wife, who came out of her hut to draw water from a gigantic pot in the shade of a small tree in the middle of the compound.

'She has gone to plait her hair.'

Okonkwo bit his lips as anger welled up within him.

'Where are her children? Did she take them?' he asked with unusual coolness and restraint.

'They are here,' answered his first wife, Nwoye's mother. Okonkwo bent down and looked into her hut. Ojiugo's children were eating with the children of his first wife.

'Did she ask you to feed them before she went?'

'Yes,' lied Nwoye's mother, trying to minimize Ojiugo's thoughtlessness.

Okonkwo knew she was not speaking the truth. He walked back to his *obi* to await Ojiugo's return. And when she returned he beat her very heavily. In his anger he had forgotten that it was the Week of Peace. His first two wives ran out in great alarm pleading with him that it was the sacred week. But Okonkwo was not the man to stop beating somebody half-way through, not even for fear of a goddess.

Okonkwo's neighbors heard his wife crying and sent their voices over the compound walls to ask what was the matter. Some of them came over to see for themselves. It was unheard of to beat somebody during the sacred week.

Before it was dusk Ezeani, who was the priest of the earth goddess, Ani, called on Okonkwo in his *obi*. Okonkwo brought out kola nut and placed it before the priest.

'Take away your kola nut. I shall not eat in the house of a man who has no respect for our gods and ancestors.'

Okonkwo tried to explain to him what his wife had

done, but Ezeani seemed to pay no attention. He held a short staff in his hand which he brought down on the floor to emphasize his points.

'Listen to me,' he said when Okonkwo had spoken. 'You are not a stranger in Umuofia. You know as well as I do that our forefathers ordained that before we plant any crops in the earth we should observe a week in which a man does not say a harsh word to his neighbor. We live in peace with our fellows to honor our great goddess of the earth without whose blessing our crops will not grow. You have committed a great evil.' He brought down his staff heavily on the floor. 'Your wife was at fault, but even if you came into your *obi* and found her lover on top of her, you would still have committed a great evil to beat her.' His staff came down again. 'The evil you have done can ruin the whole clan. The earth goddess whom you have insulted may refuse to give us her increase, and we shall all perish.' His tone now changed from anger to command. 'You will bring to the shrine of Ani tomorrow one she-goat, one hen, a length of cloth and a hundred cowries.' He rose and left the hut.

Okonkwo did as the priest said. He also took with him a pot of palm-wine. Inwardly, he was repentant. But he was not the man to go about telling his neighbors that he was in error. And so people said he had no respect for the gods of the clan. His enemies said his good fortune had gone to his head. They called him the little bird *nza* who so far forgot himself after a heavy meal that he challenged his *chi*.

No work was done during the Week of Peace. People called on their neighbors and drank palm-wine. This year they talked of nothing else but the *nso-ani* which Okonkwo had committed. It was the first time for many years that a man had broken the sacred peace. Even the oldest men could only remember one or two other occasions somewhere in the dim past.

Ogbuefi Ezeudu, who was the oldest man in the village, was telling two other men who came to visit him that the punishment for breaking the Peace of Ani had become very mild in their clan.

'It has not always been so,' he said. 'My father told me that he had been told that in the past a man who broke the peace was dragged on the ground through the village until he died. But after a while this custom was stopped because it spoiled the peace which it was meant to preserve.'

'Somebody told me yesterday,' said one of' the younger men, 'that in some clans it is an abomination for a man to die during the Week of Peace.'

'It is indeed true,' said Ogbuefi Ezeudu. 'They have that custom in Obodoani. If a man dies at this time he is not buried but cast into the Evil Forest. It is a bad custom which these people observe because they lack understanding. They throw away large numbers of men and women without burial. And what is the result? Their clan is full of the evil spirits of these unburied dead, hungry to do harm to the living.'

After the Week of Peace every man and his family began to clear the bush to make new farms. The cut bush was left to dry and fire was then set to it. As the smoke rose into the sky kites appeared from different directions and hovered over the burning field in silent valediction. The rainy season was approaching when they would go away until the dry season returned.

Okonkwo spent the next few days preparing his seed-yams. He looked at each yam carefully to see whether it was good for sowing. Sometimes he de-cided that a yam was too big to be sown as one seed and he split it deftly along its length with his sharp knife. His eldest son, Nwoye, and Ikemefuna helped him by fetching the yams in long baskets from the barn and in counting the prepared seeds in groups of four hundred. Sometimes Okonkwo gave them a few yams each to prepare. But he always found fault with their effort, and he said so with much threatening.

'Do you think you are cutting up yams for cooking?' he asked Nwoye. 'If you split another yam of this size, I shall break your jaw. You think you are still a child. I began to own a farm at your age. And you,' he said to Ikemefuna, 'do you not grow yams where you come from?'

Inwardly Okonkwo knew that the boys were still too young to understand fully the difficult art of preparing seed-yams. But he thought that one could not begin too early. Yam stood for manliness, and he who could feed his family on yams from one harvest to another was a very great man indeed. Okonkwo wanted his son to be a great farmer and a great man. He would stamp out the disquieting signs of laziness which he thought he already saw in him.

'I will not have a son who cannot hold up his head in the gathering of the clan. I would sooner strangle him with my own hands. And if you stand staring at me like that,' he swore, 'Amadiora will break your head for you!'

Some days later, when the land had been moistened by two or three heavy rains, Okonkwo and his family went to the farm with baskets of seed-yams, their hoes and machetes, and the planting began. They made single mounds of earth in straight lines all over the field and sowed the yams in them.

Yam, the king of crops, was a very exacting king. For three or four moons it demanded hard work and constant attention from cock-crow till the chickens went back to roost. The young tendrils were protected from earth-heat with rings of sisal leaves. As the rains became heavier the women planted maize, melons and beans between the yam mounds. The yams were then staked, first with little sticks and later with tall and big tree branches. The women weeded the farm three times at definite periods in the life of the yams, neither early nor late.

And now the rains had really come, so heavy and persistent that even the village rain-maker no longer claimed to be able to intervene. He could not stop the rain now, just as he would not attempt to start it in the heart of the dry season, without serious danger to his own health. The personal dynamism required to counter the forces of these extremes of weather would be far too great for the human frame.

And so nature was not interfered with in the middle of the rainy season. Sometimes it poured down in such thick sheets of water that earth and sky seemed merged in one gray wetness. It was then uncertain whether the low rumbling of Amadiora's thunder came from above or below. At such times, in each of the countless thatched huts of Umuofia, children sat around their mother's cooking fire telling stories, or with their father in his *obi* warming themselves from a long fire, roasting and eating maize. It was a brief resting period between the exacting and arduous planting season and the equally exacting but light-hearted month of harvests.

Ikemefuna had begun to feel like a member of Okonkwo's family. He still thought about his mother and his three-year-old sister, and he had moments of sadness and depression. But he and Nwoye had become so deeply attached to each other that such moments became less frequent and less poignant. Ikemefuna had an endless stock of folk tales. Even those which Nwoye knew already were told with a new freshness and the local flavor of a different clan. Nwoye remembered this period very vividly till the end of his life. He even remembered how he had laughed when Ikemefuna told him that the proper name for a corn cob with only a few scattered grains was *eze-agadi-nwayi,* or the teeth of an old woman. Nwoye's mind had gone immediately to Nwayieke, who lived near the udala tree. She had about three teeth and was always smoking her pipe.

Gradually the rains became lighter and less frequent, and earth and sky once again became separate. The rain fell in thin, slanting showers through sunshine and quiet breeze. Children no longer stayed indoors but ran about singing:

> 'The rain is falling, the sun is shining,
> Alone Nnadi is cooking and eating.'

Nwoye always wondered who Nnadi was and why he should live all by himself, cooking and eating. In the end he decided that Nnadi must live in that land of Ikemefuna's favorite story where the ant holds his court in splendor and the sands dance forever.

Five

THE Feast of the New Yam was approaching and
Umuofia was in a festival mood. It was an occasion for
giving thanks to Ani, the earth goddess and the source
of all fertility. Ani played a greater part in the life of
the people than any other deity. She was the ultimate
judge of morality and conduct. And what was more,
she was in close communion with the departed fathers
of the clan whose bodies had been committed to
earth.

The Feast of the New Yam was held every year
before the harvest began, to honor the earth goddess
and the ancestral spirits of the clan. New yams could
not be eaten until some had first been offered to these
powers. Men and women, young and old, looked forward to the New Yam Festival because it began the
season of plenty – the new year. On the last night
before the festival, yams of the old year were all dis-
posed of by those who still had them. The new year
must begin with tasty, fresh yams and not the shriveled
and fibrous crop of the previous year. All cooking
pots, calabashes and wooden bowls were thoroughly
washed, especially the wooden mortar in which
yam was pounded. Yam foo-foo and vegetable soup
was the chief food in the celebration. So much of it
was cooked that, no matter how heavily the family ate
or how many friends and relatives they invited from
neighboring villages, there was always a large quantity
of food left over at the end of the day. The story was
always told of a wealthy man who set before his guests

31

a mound of foo-foo so high that those who sat on one side could not see what was happening on the other, and it was not until late in the evening that one of them saw for the first time his in-law who had arrived during the course of the meal and had fallen to on the opposite side. It was only then that they exchanged greetings and shook hands over what was left of the food.

The New Yam Festival was thus an occasion for joy throughout Umuofia. And every man whose arm was strong, as the Ibo people say, was expected to invite large numbers of guests from far and wide. Okonkwo always asked his wives' relations, and since he now had three wives his guests would make a fairly big crowd.

But somehow Okonkwo could never become as enthusiastic over feasts as most people. He was a good eater and he could drink one or two fairly big gourds of palm-wine. But he was always uncomfortable sitting around for days waiting for a feast or getting over it. He would be very much happier working on his farm.

The festival was now only three days away. Okonkwo's wives had scrubbed the walls and the huts with red earth until they reflected light. They had then drawn patterns on them in white, yellow and dark green. They then set about painting themselves with cam wood and drawing beautiful black patterns on their stomachs and on their backs. The children were also decorated, especially their hair, which was shaved in beautiful patterns. The three women talked excitedly about the relations who had been invited, and the children reveled in the thought of being spoiled by these visitors from the motherland. Ikemefuna was equally excited. The New Yam Festival seemed to him to be a much bigger event here than in his own village, a place which was already becoming remote and vague in his imagination.

And then the storm burst. Okonkwo, who had been walking about aimlessly in his compound in suppressed anger, suddenly found an outlet.

'Who killed this banana tree?' he asked.

A hush fell on the compound immediately.

'Who killed this tree? Or are you all deaf and dumb?'

As a matter of fact the tree was very much alive. Okonkwo's second wife had merely cut a few leaves off it to wrap some food, and she said so. Without further argument Okonkwo gave her a sound beating and left her and her only daughter weeping. Neither of the other wives dared to interfere beyond an occasional and tentative, 'It is enough, Okonkwo,' pleaded from a reasonable distance.

His anger thus satisfied, Okonkwo decided to go out hunting. He had an old rusty gun made by a clever blacksmith who had come to live in Umuofia long ago. But although Okonkwo was a great man whose prowess was universally acknowledged, he was not a hunter. In fact he had not killed a rat with his gun. And so when he called Ikemefuna to fetch his gun, the wife who had just been beaten murmured something about guns that never shot. Unfortunately for her, Okonkwo heard it and ran madly into his room for the loaded gun, ran out again and aimed at her as she clambered over the dwarf wall of the barn. He pressed the trigger and there was a loud report accompanied by the wail of his wives and children. He threw down the gun and jumped into the barn, and there lay the woman, very much shaken and frightened but quite unhurt. He heaved a heavy sigh and went away with the gun.

In spite of this incident the New Yam Festival was celebrated with great joy in Okonkwo's household. Early that morning as he offered a sacrifice of new yam and palm-oil to his ancestors he asked them to protect him, his children and their mothers in the new year.

As the day wore on his in-laws arrived from three surrounding villages, and each party brought with them a huge pot of palm-wine. And there was eating and drinking till night, when Okonkwo's in-laws began to leave for their homes.

The second day of the new year was the day of the great wrestling match between Okonkwo's village and their neighbors. It was difficult to say which the people enjoyed more – the feasting and fellowship of the first day or the wrestling contest of the second. But there was one woman who had no doubt whatever in her mind. She was Okonkwo's second wife, Ekwefi, whom he nearly shot. There was no festival in all the seasons of the year which gave her as much pleasure as the wrestling match. Many years ago when she was the village beauty Okonkwo had won her heart by throwing the Cat in the greatest contest within living memory. She did not marry him then because he was too poor to pay her bride-price. But a few years later she ran away from her husband and came to live with Okonkwo. All this happened many years ago. Now Ekwefi was a woman of forty-five who had suffered a great deal in her time. But her love of wrestling contests was still as strong as it was thirty years ago.

It was not yet noon on the second day of the New Yam Festival. Ekwefi and her only daughter, Ezinma, sat near the fireplace waiting for the water in the pot to boil. The fowl Ekwefi had just killed was in the wooden mortar. The water began to boil, and in one deft movement she lifted the pot from the fire and poured the boiling water over the fowl. She put back the empty pot on the circular pad in the corner, and looked at her palms, which were black with soot. Ezinma was always surprised that her mother could lift a pot from the fire with her bare hands.

'Ekwefi,' she said, 'is it true that when people are grown up, fire does not burn them?' Ezinma, unlike most children, called her mother by her name.

'Yes,' replied Ekwefi, too busy to argue. Her daughter was only ten years old but she was wiser than her years.

'But Nwoye's mother dropped her pot of hot soup the other day and it broke on the floor.'

Ekwefi turned the hen over in the mortar and began to pluck the feathers.

'Ekwefi,' said Ezinma, who had joined in plucking the feathers, 'my eyelid is twitching.'

'It means you are going to cry,' said her mother.

'No,' Ezinma said, 'it is this eyelid, the top one.'

'That means you will see something.'

'What will I see?' she asked.

'How can I know?' Ekwefi wanted her to work it out herself.

'Oho,' said Ezinma at last. 'I know what it is – the wrestling match.'

At last the hen was plucked clean. Ekwefi tried to pull out the horny beak but it was too hard. She turned round on her low stool and put the beak in the fire for a few moments. She pulled again and it came off.

'Ekwefi!' a voice called from one of the other huts. It was Nwoye's mother, Okonkwo's first wife.

'Is that me?' Ekwefi called back. That was the way people answered calls from outside. They never answered yes for fear it might be an evil spirit calling.

'Will you give Ezinma some fire to bring to me?' Her own children and Ikemefuna had gone to the stream.

Ekwefi put a few live coals into a piece of broken pot and Ezinma carried it across the clean swept compound to Nwoye's mother.

'Thank you, Nma,' she said. She was peeling new yams, and in a basket beside her were green vegetables and beans.

'Let me make the fire for you,' Ezinma offered.

'Thank you, Ezigbo,' she said. She often called her Ezigbo, which means 'the good one.'

Ezinma went outside and brought some sticks from a huge bundle of firewood. She broke them into little pieces across the sole of her foot and began to build a fire, blowing it with her breath.

'You will blow your eyes out,' said Nwoye's mother, looking up from the yams she was peeling. 'Use the fan.' She stood up and pulled out the fan which was fastened into one of the rafters. As soon as she got up, the troublesome nanny-goat, which had been dutifully eating yam peelings, dug her teeth into the real thing, scooped out two mouthfuls and fled from the hut to chew the cud in the goats' shed. Nwoye's mother swore at her and settled down again to her peeling. Ezinma's fire was now sending up thick clouds of smoke. She went on fanning it until it burst into flames. Nwoye's mother thanked her and she went back to her mother's hut.

Just then the distant beating of drums began to reach them. It came from the direction of the *ilo*, the village playground. Every village had its own *ilo* which was as old as the village itself and where all the great ceremonies and dances took place. The drums beat the unmistakable wrestling dance – quick, light and gay, and it came floating on the wind.

Okonkwo cleared his throat and moved his feet to the beat of the drums. It filled him with fire as it had always done from his youth. He trembled with the desire to conquer and subdue. It was like the desire for woman.

'We shall be late for the wrestling,' said Ezinma to her mother.

'They will not begin until the sun goes down.'

'But they are beating the drums.'

'Yes. The drums begin at noon but the wrestling waits until the sun begins to sink. Go and see if your father has brought out yams for the afternoon.'

'He has. Nwoye's mother is already cooking.'

'Go and bring our own, then. We must cook quickly or we shall be late for the wrestling.'

Ezinma ran in the direction of the barn and brought back two yams from the dwarf wall.

Ekwefi peeled the yams quickly. The troublesome nanny-goat sniffed about, eating the peelings. She cut the yams into small pieces and began to prepare a pottage, using some of the chicken.

At that moment they heard someone crying just outside their compound. It was very much like Obiageli, Nwoye's sister.

'Is that not Obiageli weeping?' Ekwefi called across the yard to Nwoye's mother.

'Yes,' she replied. 'She must have broken her water-pot.'

The weeping was now quite close and soon the children filed in, carrying on their heads various sizes of pots suitable to their years. Ikemefuna came first with the biggest pot, closely followed by Nwoye and his two younger brothers. Obiageli brought up the rear, her face streaming with tears. In her hand was the cloth pad on which the pot should have rested on her head.

'What happened?' her mother asked, and Obiageli told her mournful story. Her mother consoled her and promised to buy her another pot.

CHINUA ACHEBE

Nwoye's younger brothers were about to tell their mother the true story of the accident when Ikemefuna looked at them sternly and they held their peace. The fact was that Obiageli had been making *inyanga* with her pot. She had balanced it on her head, folded her arms in front of her and began to sway her waist like a grown-up young lady. When the pot fell down and broke she burst out laughing. She only began to weep when they got near the iroko tree outside their compound.

The drums were still beating, persistent and unchanging. Their sound was no longer a separate thing from the living village. It was like the pulsation of its heart. It throbbed in the air, in the sunshine, and even in the trees, and filled the village with excitement.

Ekwefi ladled her husband's share of the pottage into a bowl and covered it. Ezinma took it to him in his *obi*.

Okonkwo was sitting on a goatskin already eating his first wife's meal. Obiageli, who had brought it from her mother's hut, sat on the floor waiting for him to finish. Ezinma placed her mother's dish before him and sat with Obiageli.

'Sit like a woman!' Okonkwo shouted at her. Ezinma brought her two legs together and stretched them in front of her.

'Father, will you go to see the wrestling?' Ezinma asked after a suitable interval.

'Yes,' he answered. 'Will you go?'

'Yes.' And after a pause she said: 'Can I bring your chair for you?'

'No, that is a boy's job.' Okonkwo was specially fond of Ezinma. She looked very much like her mother, who was once the village beauty. But his fondness only showed on very rare occasions.

'Obiageli broke her pot today,' Ezinma said.

38

'Yes, she has told me about it,' Okonkwo said between mouthfuls.

'Father,' said Obiageli, 'people should not talk when they are eating or pepper may go down the wrong way.'

'That is very true. Do you hear that, Ezinma? You are older than Obiageli but she has more sense.'

He uncovered his second wife's dish and began to eat from it. Obiageli took the first dish and returned to her mother's hut. And then Nkechi came in, bringing the third dish. Nkechi was the daughter of Okonkwo's third wife.

In the distance the drums continued to beat.

Six

THE whole village turned out on the *ilo*, men, women and children. They stood round in a huge circle leaving the center of the playground free. The elders and grandees of the village sat on their own stools brought there by their young sons or slaves. Okonkwo was among them. All others stood except those who came early enough to secure places on the few stands which had been built by placing smooth logs on forked pillars.

The wrestlers were not there yet and the drummers held the field. They too sat just in front of the huge circle of spectators, facing the elders. Behind them was the big and ancient silk-cotton tree which was sacred. Spirits of good children lived in that tree waiting to be born. On ordinary days young women who desired children came to sit under its shade.

There were seven drums and they were arranged according to their sizes in a long wooden basket. Three men beat them with sticks, working feverishly from one drum to another. They were possessed by the spirit of the drums.

The young men who kept order on these occasions dashed about, consulting among themselves and with the leaders of the two wrestling teams, who were still outside the circle, behind the crowd. Once in a while two young men carrying palm fronds ran round the circle and kept the crowd back by beating the ground in front of them or, if they were stubborn, their legs and feet.

At last the two teams danced into the circle and the

crowd roared and clapped. The drums rose to a frenzy. The people surged forward. The young men who kept order flew around, waving their palm fronds. Old men nodded to the beat of the drums and remembered the days when they wrestled to its intoxicating rhythm.

The contest began with boys of fifteen or sixteen. There were only three such boys in each team. They were not the real wrestlers; they merely set the scene. Within a short time the first two bouts were over. But the third created a big sensation even among the elders who did not usually show their excitement so openly. It was as quick as the other two, perhaps even quicker. But very few people had ever seen that kind of wrestling before. As soon as the two boys closed in, one of them did something which no one could describe because it had been as quick as a flash. And the other boy was flat on his back. The crowd roared and clapped and for a while drowned the frenzied drums. Okonkwo sprang to his feet and quickly sat down again. Three young men from the victorious boy's team ran forward, carried him shoulder high and danced through the cheering crowd. Everybody soon knew who the boy was. His name was Maduka, the son of Obierika.

The drummers stopped for a brief rest before the real matches. Their bodies shone with sweat, and they took up fans and began to fan themselves. They also drank water from small pots and ate kola nuts. They became ordinary human beings again, talking and laughing among themselves and with others who stood near them. The air, which had been stretched taut with excitement, relaxed again. It was as if water had been poured on the tightened skin of a drum. Many people looked around, perhaps for the first time, and saw those who stood or sat next to them.

'I did not know it was you,' Ekwefi said to the woman who had stood shoulder to shoulder with her since the beginning of the matches.

'I do not blame you,' said the woman. 'I have never seen such a large crowd of people. Is it true that Okonkwo nearly killed you with his gun?'

'It is true indeed, my dear friend. I cannot yet find a mouth with which to tell the story.'

'Your *chi* is very much awake, my friend. And how is my daughter, Ezinma?'

'She has been very well for some time now. Perhaps she has come to stay.'

'I think she has. How old is she now?'

'She is about ten years old.'

'I think she will stay. They usually stay if they do not die before the age of six.'

'I pray she stays,' said Ekwefi with a heavy sigh.

The woman with whom she talked was called Chielo. She was the priestess of Agbala, the Oracle of the Hills and the Caves. In ordinary life Chielo was a widow with two children. She was very friendly with Ekwefi and they shared a common shed in the market. She was particularly fond of Ekwefi's only daughter, Ezinma, whom she called 'my daughter.' Quite often she bought beancakes and gave Ekwefi some to take home to Ezinma. Anyone seeing Chielo in ordinary life would hardly believe she was the same person who prophesied when the spirit of Agbala was upon her.

The drummers took up their sticks and the air shivered and grew tense like a tightened bow.

The two teams were ranged facing each other across the clear space. A young man from one team danced across the center to the other side and pointed at whomever he wanted to fight. They danced back to the center together and then closed in.

There were twelve men on each side and the challenge went from one side to the other. Two judges walked around the wrestlers and when they thought they were equally matched, stopped them. Five matches ended in this way. But the really exciting moments were when a man was thrown. The huge voice of the crowd then rose to the sky and in every direction. It was even heard in the surrounding villages.

The last match was between the leaders of the teams. They were among the best wrestlers in all the nine villages. The crowd wondered who would throw the other this year. Some said Okafo was the better man; others said he was not the equal of Ikezue. Last year neither of them had thrown the other even though the judges had allowed the contest to go on longer than was the custom. They had the same style and one saw the other's plans beforehand. It might happen again this year.

Dusk was already approaching when their contest began. The drums went mad and the crowds also. They surged forward as the two young men danced into the circle. The palm fronds were helpless in keeping them back.

Ikezue held out his right hand. Okafo seized it, and they closed in. It was a fierce contest. Ikezue strove to dig in his right heel behind Okafo so as to pitch him backwards in the clever *ege* style. But the one knew what the other was thinking. The crowd had surrounded and swallowed up the drummers, whose frantic rhythm was no longer a mere disembodied sound but the very heartbeat of the people.

The wrestlers were now almost still in each other's grip. The muscles on their arms and their thighs and on their backs stood out and twitched. It looked like an equal match. The two judges were already moving forward to separate them when Ikezue, now desperate, went down quickly on one knee in an attempt to fling his man backwards over his head. It was a sad miscalculation. Quick as the lightning of Amadiora, Okafo raised his right leg and swung it over his rival's head. The crowd burst into a thunderous roar. Okafo was swept off his feet by his supporters and carried home shoulder high. They sang his praise and the young women clapped their hands:

> 'Who will wrestle for our village?
>   Okafo will wrestle for our village.
> Has he thrown a hundred men?
>   He has thrown four hundred men.
> Has he thrown a hundred Cats?
>   He has thrown four hundred Cats.
> Then send him word to fight for us.'

Seven

FOR three years Ikemefuna lived in Okonkwo's household and the elders of Umuofia seemed to have forgotten about him. He grew rapidly like a yam tendril in the rainy season, and was full of the sap of life. He had become wholly absorbed into his new family. He was like an elder brother to Nwoye, and from the very first seemed to have kindled a new fire in the younger boy. He made him feel grown-up; and they no longer spent the evenings in mother's hut while she cooked, but now sat with Okonkwo in his *obi*, or watched him as he tapped his palm tree for the evening wine. Nothing pleased Nwoye now more than to be sent for by his mother or another of his father's wives to do one of those difficult and masculine tasks in the home, like splitting wood, or pounding food. On receiving such a message through a younger brother or sister, Nwoye would feign annoyance and grumble aloud about women and their troubles.

Okonkwo was inwardly pleased at his son's development, and he knew it was due to Ikemefuna. He wanted Nwoye to grow into a tough young man capable of ruling his father's household when he was dead and gone to join the ancestors. He wanted him to be a prosperous man, having enough in his barn to feed the ancestors with regular sacrifices. And so he was always happy when he heard him grumbling about women. That showed that in time he would be able to control his women-folk. No matter how prosperous a man was, if he was unable to rule his women and his children (and especially his women) he was not really a man. He was like the man in the song who had ten and one wives and not enough soup for his foo-foo.

So Okonkwo encouraged the boys to sit with him in his *obi*, and he told them stories of the land – masculine stories of violence and bloodshed. Nwoye knew that it was right to be masculine and to be violent, but somehow he still preferred the stories that his mother used to tell, and which she no doubt still told to her younger children – stories of the tortoise and his wily ways, and of the bird *eneke-nti-oba* who challenged the whole world to a wrestling contest and was finally thrown by the cat. He remembered the story she often told of the quarrel between Earth and Sky long ago, and how Sky withheld rain for seven years, until crops withered and the dead could not be buried because the hoes broke on the stony Earth. At last Vulture was sent to plead with Sky, and to soften his heart with a song of the suffering of the sons of men. Whenever Nwoye's mother sang this song he felt carried away to the distant scene in the sky where Vulture, Earth's emissary, sang for mercy. At last Sky was moved to pity, and he gave to Vulture rain wrapped in leaves of coco-yam. But as he flew home his long talon pierced the leaves and the rain fell as it had never fallen before. And so heavily did it rain on Vulture that he did not return to deliver his message but flew to a distant land, from where he had espied a fire. And when he got there he found it was a man making a sacrifice. He warmed himself in the fire and ate the entrails.

That was the kind of story that Nwoye loved. But he now knew that they were for foolish women and children, and he knew that his father wanted him to be a man. And so he feigned that he no longer cared for women's stories. And when he did this he saw that his father was pleased, and no longer rebuked him or beat him. So Nwoye and Ikemefuna would listen to Okonkwo's stories about tribal wars, or how, years ago, he had stalked his victim, overpowered him and obtained his first human head. And as he told them of the past they sat in darkness or the dim glow of logs, waiting for the women to finish their cooking. When they finished, each brought her bowl of foo-foo and bowl of soup to her husband. An oil lamp was lit and Okonkwo tasted from each bowl, and then passed two shares to Nwoye and Ikemefuna.

In this way the moons and the seasons passed. And then the locusts came. It had not happened for many a long year. The elders said locusts came once in a generation, reappeared every year for seven years and then disappeared for another lifetime. They went back to their caves in a distant land, where they were guarded by a race of stunted men. And then after another lifetime these men opened the caves again and the locusts came to Umuofia.

They came in the cold harmattan season after the harvests had been gathered, and ate up all the wild grass in the fields.

Okonkwo and the two boys were working on the red outer walls of the compound. This was one of the lighter tasks of the after-harvest season. A new cover of thick palm branches and palm leaves was set on the walls to protect them from the next rainy season. Okonkwo worked on the outside of the wall and the boys worked from within. There were little holes from one side to the other in the upper levels of the wall, and through these Okonkwo passed the rope, or *tie-tie*, to the boys and they passed it round the wooden stays and then back to him; and in this way the cover was strengthened on the wall.

The women had gone to the bush to collect fire-wood, and the little children to visit their playmates in the neighboring compounds. The harmattan was in the air and seemed to distill a hazy feeling of sleep on the world. Okonkwo and the boys worked in complete silence, which was only broken when a new palm frond was lifted on to the wall or when a busy hen moved dry leaves about in her ceaseless search for food.

And then quite suddenly a shadow fell on the world, and the sun seemed hidden behind a thick cloud. Okonkwo looked up from his work and wondered if it was going to rain at such an unlikely time of the year. But almost immediately a shout of joy broke out in all directions, and Umuofia, which had dozed in the noon-day haze, broke into life and activity.

'Locusts are descending,' was joyfully chanted everywhere, and men, women and children left their work or their play and ran into the open to see the unfamiliar sight. The locusts had not come for many, many years, and only the old people had seen them before.

At first, a fairly small swarm came. They were the harbingers sent to survey the land. And then appeared on the horizon a slowly-moving mass like a boundless sheet of black cloud drifting towards Umuofia. Soon it covered half the sky, and the solid mass was now broken by tiny eyes of light like shining star dust. It was a tremendous sight, full of power and beauty.

Everyone was now about, talking excitedly and praying that the locusts should camp in Umuofia for the night. For although locusts had not visited Umuofia for many years, everybody knew by instinct that they were very good to eat. And at last the locusts did descend. They settled on every tree and on every blade of grass; they settled on the roofs and covered the bare ground. Mighty tree branches broke away under them, and the whole country became the brown-earth color of the vast, hungry swarm.

Many people went out with baskets trying to catch them, but the elders counseled patience till nightfall. And they were right. The locusts settled in the bushes for the night and their wings became wet with dew. Then all Umuofia turned out in spite of the cold harmattan, and everyone filled his bags and pots with locusts. The next morning they were roasted in clay pots and then spread in the sun until they became dry and brittle. And for many days this rare food was eaten with solid palm-oil.

Okonkwo sat in his *obi* crunching happily with Ikemefuna and Nwoye, and drinking palm-wine copiously, when Ogbuefi Ezeudu came in. Ezeudu was the oldest man in this quarter of Umuofia. He had been a great and fearless warrior in his time, and was now accorded great respect in all the clan. He refused to join in the meal, and asked Okonkwo to have a word with him outside. And so they walked out together, the old man supporting himself with his stick. When they were out of earshot, he said to Okonkwo:

'That boy calls you father. Do not bear a hand in his death.' Okonkwo was surprised, and was about to say something when the old man continued:

'Yes, Umuofia has decided to kill him. The Oracle of the Hills and the Caves has pronounced it. They will take him outside Umuofia as is the custom, and kill him there. But I want you to have nothing to do with it. He calls you his father.'

The next day a group of elders from all the nine villages of Umuofia came to Okonkwo's house early in the morning, and before they began to speak in low tones Nwoye and Ikemefuna were sent out. They did not stay very long, but when they went away Okonkwo sat still for a very long time supporting his chin in his palms. Later in the day he called Ikemefuna and told him that he was to be taken home the next day. Nwoye overheard it and burst into tears, whereupon his father beat him heavily. As for Ikemefuna, he was at a loss. His own home had gradually become very faint and distant. He still missed his mother and his sister and would be very glad to see them. But somehow he knew he was not going to see them. He remembered once when men had talked in low tones with his father; and it seemed now as if it was happening all over again.

Later, Nwoye went to his mother's hut and told her that Ikemefuna was going home. She immediately dropped her pestle with which she was grinding pepper, folded her arms across her breast and sighed, 'Poor child.'

The next day, the men returned with a pot of wine. They were all fully dressed as if they were going to a big clan meeting or to pay a visit to a neighboring village. They passed their cloths under the right armpit, and hung their goatskin bags and sheathed machetes over their left shoulders. Okonkwo got ready quickly and the party set out with Ikemefuna carrying the pot of wine. A deathly silence descended on Okonkwo's compound. Even the very little children seemed to know. Throughout that day Nwoye sat in his mother's hut and tears stood in his eyes.

At the beginning of their journey the men of Umuofia talked and laughed about the locusts, about their women, and about some effeminate men who had refused to come with them. But as they drew near to the outskirts of Umuofia silence fell upon them too.

The sun rose slowly to the center of the sky, and the dry, sandy footway began to throw up the heat that lay buried in it. Some birds chirruped in the forests around. The men trod dry leaves on the sand. All else was silent. Then from the distance came the faint beating of the *ekwe*. It rose and faded with the wind – a peaceful dance from a distant clan.

'It is an *ozo* dance,' the men said among themselves. But no one was sure where it was coming from. Some said Ezimili, others Abame or Aninta. They argued for a short while and fell into silence again, and the elusive dance rose and fell with the wind. Somewhere a man was taking one of the titles of his clan, with music and dancing and a great feast.

The footway had now become a narrow line in the heart of the forest. The short trees and sparse under-growth which surrounded the men's village began to give way to giant trees and climbers which perhaps had stood from the beginning of things, untouched by the ax and the bush-fire. The sun breaking through their leaves and branches threw a pattern of light and shade on the sandy footway.

Ikemefuna heard a whisper close behind him and turned round sharply. The man who had whispered now called out aloud, urging the others to hurry up.

'We still have a long way to go,' he said. Then he and another man went before Ikemefuna and set a faster pace.

Thus the men of Umuofia pursued their way, armed with sheathed machetes, and Ikemefuna, carrying a pot of palm-wine on his head, walked in their midst. Although he had felt uneasy at first, he was not afraid now. Okonkwo walked behind him. He could hardly imagine that Okonkwo was not his real father. He had never been fond of his real father, and at the end of three years he had become very distant indeed. But

51

his mother and his three-year-old sister . . . of course she would not be three now, but six. Would he recognize her now? She must have grown quite big. How his mother would weep for joy, and thank Okonkwo for having looked after him so well and for bringing him back. She would want to hear everything that had happened to him in all these years. Could he remember them all? He would tell her about Nwoye and his mother, and about the locusts. . . . Then quite suddenly a thought came upon him. His mother might be dead. He tried in vain to force the thought out of his mind. Then he tried to settle the matter the way he used to settle such matters when he was a little boy. He still remembered the song:

> *Eze elina, elina!*
> > *Sala*
> *Eze ilikwa ya*
> *Ikwaba akwa oligholi*
> *Ebe Danda nechi eze*
> *Ebe Uzuzu nete egwu*
> > *Sala*

He sang it in his mind, and walked to its beat. If the song ended on his right foot, his mother was alive. If it ended on his left, she was dead. No, not dead, but ill. It ended on the right. She was alive and well. He sang the song again, and it ended on the left. But the second time did not count. The first voice gets to Chukwu, or God's house. That was a favorite saying of children. Ikemefuna felt like a child once more. It must be the thought of going home to his mother.

One of the men behind him cleared his throat. Ikemefuna looked back, and the man growled at him to go on and not stand looking back. The way he said it sent cold fear down Ikemefuna's back. His hands trembled vaguely on the black pot he carried. Why had Okonkwo withdrawn to the rear? Ikemefuna felt his legs melting under him. And he was afraid to look back.

As the man who had cleared his throat drew up and raised his machete, Okonkwo looked away. He heard the blow. The pot fell and broke in the sand. He heard Ikemefuna cry, 'My father, they have killed me!' as he ran towards him. Dazed with fear, Okonkwo drew his machete and cut him down. He was afraid of being thought weak.

As soon as his father walked in, that night, Nwoye knew that Ikemefuna had been killed, and something seemed to give way inside him, like the snapping of a tightened bow. He did not cry. He just hung limp. He had had the same kind of feeling not long ago, during the last harvest season. Every child loved the harvest season. Those who were big enough to carry even a few yams in a tiny basket went with grown-ups to the farm. And if they could not help in digging up the yams, they could gather firewood together for roasting the ones that would be eaten there on the farm. This roasted yam soaked in red palm-oil and eaten in the open farm was sweeter than any meal at home. It was after such a day at the farm during the last harvest that Nwoye had felt for the first time a snapping inside him like the one he now felt. They were returning home with baskets of yams from a distant farm across the stream when they heard the voice of an infant crying in the thick forest. A sudden hush had fallen on the women, who had been talking, and they had quickened their steps. Nwoye had heard that twins were put in earthenware pots and thrown away in the forest, but he had never yet come across them. A vague chill had descended on him and his head had seemed to swell, like a solitary walker at night who passes an evil spirit on the way. Then something had given way inside him. It descended on him again, this feeling, when his father walked in, that night after killing Ikemefuna.

Eight

OKONKWO did not taste any food for two days after the death of Ikemefuna. He drank palm-wine from morning till night, and his eyes were red and fierce like the eyes of a rat when it was caught by the tail and dashed against the floor. He called his son, Nwoye, to sit with him in his *obi*. But the boy was afraid of him and slipped out of the hut as soon as he noticed him dozing.

He did not sleep at night. He tried not to think about Ikemefuna, but the more he tried the more he thought about him. Once he got up from bed and walked about his compound. But he was so weak that his legs could hardly carry him. He felt like a drunken giant walking with the limbs of a mosquito. Now and then a cold shiver descended on his head and spread down his body.

On the third day he asked his second wife, Ekwefi, to roast plantains for him. She prepared it the way he liked – with slices of oil-bean and fish.

'You have not eaten for two days,' said his daughter Ezinma when she brought the food to him. 'So you must finish this.' She sat down and stretched her legs in front of her. Okonkwo ate the food absent-mindedly. 'She should have been a boy,' he thought as he looked at his ten-year-old daughter. He passed her a piece of fish.

'Go and bring me some cold water,' he said. Ezinma rushed out of the hut, chewing the fish, and soon returned with a bowl of cool water from the earthen pot in her mother's hut.

Okonkwo took the bowl from her and gulped the water down. He ate a few more pieces of plantain and pushed the dish aside.

'Bring me my bag,' he asked, and Ezinma brought his goatskin bag from the far end of the hut. He searched in it for his snuff-bottle. It was a deep bag and took almost the whole length of his arm. It contained other things apart from his snuff-bottle. There was a drinking horn in it, and also a drinking gourd, and they knocked against each other as he searched. When he brought out the snuff-bottle he tapped it a few times against his knee-cap before taking out some snuff on the palm of his left hand. Then he remembered that he had not taken out his snuff-spoon. He searched his bag again and brought out a small, flat, ivory spoon, with which he carried the brown snuff to his nostrils.

Ezinma took the dish in one hand and the empty water bowl in the other and went back to her mother's hut. 'She should have been a boy,' Okonkwo said to himself again. His mind went back to Ikemefuna and he shivered. If only he could find some work to do he would be able to forget. But it was the season of rest between the harvest and the next planting season. The only work that men did at this time was covering the walls of their compound with new palm fronds. And Okonkwo had already done that. He had finished it on the very day the locusts came, when he had worked on one side of the wall and Ikemefuna and Nwoye on the other.

'When did you become a shivering old woman,' Okonkwo asked himself, 'you, who are known in all the nine villages for your valor in war? How can a man who has killed five men in battle fall to pieces because he has added a boy to their number? Okonkwo, you have become a woman indeed.'

He sprang to his feet, hung his goatskin bag on his shoulder and went to visit his friend, Obierika.

Obierika was sitting outside under the shade of an orange tree making thatches from leaves of the raffia-palm. He exchanged greetings with Okonkwo and led the way into his *obi*.

'I was coming over to see you as soon as I finished that thatch,' he said, rubbing off the grains of sand that clung to his thighs.

'Is it well?' Okonkwo asked.

'Yes,' replied Obierika. 'My daughter's suitor is coming today and I hope we will clinch the matter of the bride-price. I want you to be there.'

Just then Obierika's son, Maduka, came into the *obi* from outside, greeted Okonkwo and turned towards the compound.

'Come and shake hands with me,' Okonkwo said to the lad. 'Your wrestling the other day gave me much happiness.' The boy smiled, shook hands with Okonkwo and went into the compound.

'He will do great things,' Okonkwo said. 'If I had a son like him I should be happy. I am worried about Nwoye. A bowl of pounded yams can throw him in a wrestling match. His two younger brothers are more promising. But I can tell you, Obierika, that my children do not resemble me. Where are the young suckers that will grow when the old banana tree dies? If Ezinma had been a boy I would have been happier. She has the right spirit.'

'You worry yourself for nothing,' said Obierika. 'The children are still very young.'

'Nwoye is old enough to impregnate a woman. At his age I was already fending for myself. No, my friend, he is not too young. A chick that will grow into a cock can be spotted the very day it hatches. I have done my best to make Nwoye grow into a man, but there is too much of his mother in him.'

CHINUA ACHEBE

'Too much of his grandfather,' Obierika thought, but he did not say it. The same thought also came to Okonkwo's mind. But he had long learned how to lay that ghost. Whenever the thought of his father's weakness and failure troubled him he expelled it by thinking about his own strength and success. And so he did now. His mind went to his latest show of manliness.

'I cannot understand why you refused to come with us to kill that boy,' he asked Obierika.

'Because I did not want to,' Obierika replied sharply. 'I had something better to do.'

'You sound as if you question the authority and the decision of the Oracle, who said he should die.'

'I do not. Why should I? But the Oracle did not ask me to carry out its decision.'

'But someone had to do it. If we were all afraid of blood, it would not be done. And what do you think the Oracle would do then?'

'You know very well, Okonkwo, that I am not afraid of blood; and if anyone tells you that I am, he is telling a lie. And let me tell you one thing, my friend. If I were you I would have stayed at home. What you have done will not please the Earth. It is the kind of action for which the goddess wipes out whole families.'

'The Earth cannot punish me for obeying her messenger,' Okonkwo said. 'A child's fingers are not scalded by a piece of hot yam which its mother puts into its palm.'

'That is true,' Obierika agreed. 'But if the Oracle said that my son should be killed I would neither dispute it nor be the one to do it.'

They would have gone on arguing had Ofoedu not come in just then. It was clear from his twinkling eyes that he had important news. But it would be impolite

58

to rush him. Obierika offered him a lobe of the kola nut he had broken with Okonkwo. Ofoedu ate slowly and talked about the locusts. When he finished his kola nut he said:

'The things that happen these days are very strange.'

'What has happened?' asked Okonkwo.

'Do you know Ogbuefi Ndulue?' Ofoedu asked.

'Ogbuefi Ndulue of Ire village,' Okonkwo and Obierika said together.

'He died this morning,' said Ofoedu.

'That is not strange. He was the oldest man in Ire,' said Obierika.

'You are right,' Ofoedu agreed. 'But you ought to ask why the drum has not beaten to tell Umuofia of his death.'

'Why?' asked Obierika and Okonkwo together.

'That is the strange part of it. You know his first wife who walks with a stick?'

'Yes. She is called Ozoemena.'

'That is so,' said Ofoedu. 'Ozoemena was, as you know, too old to attend Ndulue during his illness. His younger wives did that. When he died this morning, one of these women went to Ozoemena's hut and told her. She rose from her mat, took her stick and walked over to the *obi*. She knelt on her knees and hands at the threshold and called her husband, who was laid on a mat. "Ogbuefi Ndulue," she called, three times, and went back to her hut. When the youngest wife went to call her again to be present at the washing of the body, she found her lying on the mat, dead.'

'That is very strange, indeed,' said Okonkwo. 'They will put off Ndulue's funeral until his wife has been buried.'

'That is why the drum has not been beaten to tell Umuofia.'

'It was always said that Ndulue and Ozoemena had one mind,' said Obierika. 'I remember when I was a young boy there was a song about them. He could not do anything without telling her.'

'I did not know that,' said Okonkwo. 'I thought he was a strong man in his youth.'

'He was indeed,' said Ofoedu.

Okonkwo shook his head doubtfully.

'He led Umuofia to war in those days,' said Obierika.

Okonkwo was beginning to feel like his old self again. All that he required was something to occupy his mind. If he had killed Ikemefuna during the busy planting season or harvesting it would not have been so bad; his mind would have been centered on his work. Okonkwo was not a man of thought but of action. But in absence of work, talking was the next best.

Soon after Ofoedu left, Okonkwo took up his goat-skin bag to go.

'I must go home to tap my palm trees for the afternoon,' he said.

'Who taps your tall trees for you?' asked Obierika.

'Umezulike,' replied Okonkwo.

'Sometimes I wish I had not taken the *ozo* title,' said Obierika. 'It wounds my heart to see these young men killing palm trees in the name of tapping.'

'It is so indeed,' Okonkwo agreed. 'But the law of the land must be obeyed.'

'I don't know how we got that law,' said Obierika. 'In many other clans a man of title is not forbidden to climb the palm tree. Here we say he cannot climb the tall tree but he can tap the short ones standing on the ground. It is like Dimaragana, who would not lend his knife for cutting up dog-meat because the dog was taboo to him, but offered to use his teeth.'

'I think it is good that our clan holds the *ozo* title in high esteem,' said Okonkwo. 'In those other clans you speak of, *ozo* is so low that every beggar takes it.'

'I was only speaking in jest,' said Obierika. 'In Abame and Aninta the title is worth less than two cowries. Every man wears the thread of title on his ankle, and does not lose it even if he steals.'

'They have indeed soiled the name of *ozo*,' said Okonkwo as he rose to go.

'It will not be very long now before my in-laws come,' said Obierika.

'I shall return very soon,' said Okonkwo, looking at the position of the sun.

There were seven men in Obierika's hut when Okonkwo returned. The suitor was a young man of about twenty-five, and with him were his father and uncle. On Obierika's side were his two elder brothers and Maduka, his sixteen-year-old son.

'Ask Akueke's mother to send us some kola nuts,' said Obierika to his son. Maduka vanished into the compound like lightning. The conversation at once centered on him, and everybody agreed that he was as sharp as a razor.

'I sometimes think he is too sharp,' said Obierika, somewhat indulgently. 'He hardly ever walks. He is always in a hurry. If you are sending him on an errand he flies away before he has heard half of the message.'

'You were very much like that yourself,' said his eldest brother. 'As our people say, "When mother-cow is chewing grass its young ones watch its mouth." Maduka has been watching your mouth.'

As he was speaking the boy returned, followed by

Akueke, his half-sister, carrying a wooden dish with three kola nuts and alligator pepper. She gave the dish to her father's eldest brother and then shook hands, very shyly, with her suitor and his relatives. She was about sixteen and just ripe for marriage. Her suitor and his relatives surveyed her young body with expert eyes as if to assure themselves that she was beautiful and ripe.

She wore a coiffure which was done up into a crest in the middle of the head. Cam wood was rubbed lightly into her skin, and all over her body were black patterns drawn with *uli*. She wore a black necklace which hung down in three coils just above her full, succulent breasts. On her arms were red and yellow bangles, and on her waist four or five rows of *jigida*, or waist beads.

When she had shaken hands, or rather held out her hand to be shaken, she returned to her mother's hut to help with the cooking.

'Remove your *jigida* first,' her mother warned as she moved near the fireplace to bring the pestle resting against the wall. 'Every day I tell you that *jigida* and fire are not friends. But you will never hear. You grew your ears for decoration, not for hearing. One of these days your *jigida* will catch fire on your waist, and then you will know.'

Akueke moved to the other end of the hut and began to remove the waist-beads. It had to be done slowly and carefully, taking each string separately, else it would break and the thousand tiny rings would have to be strung together again. She rubbed each string downwards with her palms until it passed the buttocks and slipped down to the floor around her feet.

The men in the *obi* had already begun to drink the palm-wine which Akueke's suitor had brought. It was a very good wine and powerful, for in spite of the palm fruit hung across the mouth of the pot to restrain the lively liquor, white foam rose and spilled over.

'That wine is the work of a good tapper,' said Okonkwo.

The young suitor, whose name was Ibe, smiled broadly and said to his father: 'Do you hear that?' He then said to the others: 'He will never admit that I am a good tapper.'

'He tapped three of my best palm trees to death,' said his father, Ukegbu.

'That was about five years ago,' said Ibe, who had begun to pour out the wine, 'before I learned how to tap.' He filled the first horn and gave to his father. Then he poured out for the others. Okonkwo brought out his big horn from the goatskin bag, blew into it to remove any dust that might be there, and gave it to Ibe to fill.

As the men drank, they talked about everything except the thing for which they had gathered. It was only after the pot had been emptied that the suitor's father cleared his voice and announced the object of their visit.

Obierika then presented to him a small bundle of short broomsticks. Ukegbu counted them.

'They are thirty?' he asked.

Obierika nodded in agreement.

'We are at last getting somewhere,' Ukegbu said, and then turning to his brother and his son he said: 'Let us go out and whisper together.' The three rose and went outside. When they returned Ukegbu handed the bundle of sticks back to Obierika. He counted them; instead of thirty there were now only fifteen. He passed them over to his eldest brother, Machi, who also counted them and said:

'We had not thought to go below thirty. But as the dog said, "If I fall down for you and you fall down for

63

me, it is play". Marriage should be a play and not a fight; so we are falling down again.' He then added ten sticks to the fifteen and gave the bundle to Ukegbu.

In this way Akueke's bride-price was finally settled at twenty bags of cowries. It was already dusk when the two parties came to this agreement.

'Go and tell Akueke's mother that we have finished,' Obierika said to his son, Maduka. Almost immediately the woman came in with a big bowl of foo-foo. Obierika's second wife followed with a pot of soup, and Maduka brought in a pot of palm-wine.

As the men ate and drank palm-wine they talked about the customs of their neighbors.

'It was only this morning,' said Obierika, 'that Okonkwo and I were talking about Abame and Aninta, where titled men climb trees and pound foo-foo for their wives.'

'All their customs are upside-down. They do not decide bride-price as we do, with sticks. They haggle and bargain as if they were buying a goat or a cow in the market.'

'That is very bad,' said Obierika's eldest brother. 'But what is good in one place is bad in another place. In Umunso they do not bargain at all, not even with broomsticks. The suitor just goes on bringing bags of cowries until his in-laws tell him to stop. It is a bad custom because it always leads to a quarrel.'

'The world is large,' said Okonkwo. 'I have even heard that in some tribes a man's children belong to his wife and her family.'

'That cannot be,' said Machi. 'You might as well say that the woman lies on top of the man when they are making the children.'

'It is like the story of white men who, they say, are white like this piece of chalk,' said Obierika. He held

64

up a piece of chalk, which every man kept in his *obi* and with which his guests drew lines on the floor before they ate kola nuts. 'And these white men, they say, have no toes.'

'And have you never seen them?' asked Machi.

'Have you?' asked Obierika.

'One of them passes here frequently,' said Machi. 'His name is Amadi.'

Those who knew Amadi laughed. He was a leper, and the polite name for leprosy was 'the white skin.'

Nine

FOR the first time in three nights, Okonkwo slept. He woke up once in the middle of the night and his mind went back to the past three days without making him feel uneasy. He began to wonder why he had felt uneasy at all. It was like a man wondering in broad daylight why a dream had appeared so terrible to him at night. He stretched himself and scratched his thigh where a mosquito had bitten him as he slept. Another one was wailing near his right ear. He slapped the ear and hoped he had killed it. Why do they always go for one's ears? When he was a child his mother had told him a story about it. But it was as silly as all women's stories. Mosquito, she had said, had asked Ear to marry him, whereupon Ear fell on the floor in uncontrollable laughter. 'How much longer do you think you will live?' she asked. 'You are already a skeleton.' Mosquito went away humiliated, and any time he passed her way he told Ear that he was still alive.

Okonkwo turned on his side and went back to sleep. He was roused in the morning by someone banging on his door.

'Who is that?' he growled. He knew it must be Ekwefi. Of his three wives Ekwefi was the only one who would have the audacity to bang on his door.

'Ezinma is dying,' came her voice, and all the tragedy and sorrow of her life were packed in those words.

Okonkwo sprang from his bed, pushed back the bolt on his door and ran into Ekwefi's hut.

Ezinma lay shivering on a mat beside a huge fire that her mother had kept burning all night.

'It is *iba*,' said Okonkwo as he took his machete and went into the bush to collect the leaves and grasses and barks of trees that went into making the medicine for *iba*.

Ekwefi knelt beside the sick child, occasionally feeling with her palm the wet, burning forehead.

Ezinma was an only child and the center of her mother's world. Very often it was Ezinma who decided what food her mother should prepare. Ekwefi even gave her such delicacies as eggs, which children were rarely allowed to eat because such food tempted them to steal. One day as Ezinma was eating an egg Okonkwo had come in unexpectedly from his hut. He was greatly shocked and swore to beat Ekwefi if she dared to give the child eggs again. But it was impossible to refuse Ezinma anything. After her father's rebuke she developed an even keener appetite for eggs. And she enjoyed above all the secrecy in which she now ate them. Her mother always took her into their bedroom and shut the door.

Ezinma did not call her mother *Nne* like all children. She called her by her name, Ekwefi, as her father and other grown-up people did. The relationship between them was not only that of mother and child. There was something in it like the companionship of equals, which was strengthened by such little conspiracies as eating eggs in the bedroom.

Ekwefi had suffered a good deal in her life. She had borne ten children and nine of them had died in infancy, usually before the age of three. As she buried one child after another her sorrow gave way to despair and then to grim resignation. The birth of her children, which should be a woman's crowning glory, became for Ekwefi mere physical agony devoid of promise. The naming ceremony after seven market weeks became an empty ritual. Her deepening despair found expression in the names she gave her children. One of them was a pathetic cry, Onwumbiko – 'Death, I implore you.' But Death took no notice; Onwumbiko died in his fifteenth month. The next child was a girl, Ozoemena – 'May it not happen again.' She died in her eleventh month, and two others after her. Ekwefi then became defiant and called her next child Onwuma – 'Death may please himself.' And he did.

After the death of Ekwefi's second child, Okonkwo had gone to a medicine man, who was also a diviner of the Afa Oracle, to inquire what was amiss. This man told him that the child was an *ogbanje*, one of those wicked children who, when they died, entered their mothers' wombs to be born again.

'When your wife becomes pregnant again,' he said, 'let her not sleep in her hut. Let her go and stay with her people. In that way she will elude her wicked tormentor and break its evil cycle of birth and death.'

Ekwefi did as she was asked. As soon as she became pregnant she went to live with her old mother in another village. It was there that her third child was born and circumcized on the eighth day. She did not return to Okonkwo's compound until three days before the naming ceremony. The child was called Onwumbiko.

Onwumbiko was not given proper burial when he died. Okonkwo had called in another medicine man who was famous in the clan for his great knowledge about *ogbanje* children. His name was Okagbue Uyanwa. Okagbue was a very striking figure, tall, with a full beard and a bald head. He was light in complexion and his eyes were red and fiery. He always gnashed his teeth as he listened to those who came to consult him. He asked Okonkwo a few questions about the dead child. All the neighbors and relations who had come to mourn gathered round them.

'On what market-day was it born?' he asked.

'*Oye*,' replied Okonkwo.

'And it died this morning?'

Okonkwo said yes, and only then realized for the first time that the child had died on the same market-day as it had been born. The neighbors and relations also saw the coincidence and said among themselves that it was very significant.

'Where do you sleep with your wife, in your *obi* or in her own hut?' asked the medicine man.

'In her hut.'

'In future call her into your *obi*.'

The medicine man then ordered that there should be no mourning for the dead child. He brought out a sharp razor from the goatskin bag slung from his left shoulder and began to mutilate the child. Then he took it away to bury in the Evil Forest, holding it by the ankle and dragging it on the ground behind him. After such treatment it would think twice before coming again, unless it was one of the stubborn ones who returned, carrying the stamp of their muti-lation – a missing finger or perhaps a dark line where the medicine man's razor had cut them.

By the time Onwumbiko died Ekwefi had become a very bitter woman. Her husband's first wife had already had three sons, all strong and healthy. When she had borne her third son in succession, Okonkwo had gathered a goat for her, as was the custom. Ekwefi had nothing but good wishes for her. But she had grown so bitter about her own *chi* that she could not rejoice with others over their good fortune. And so, on the day that Nwoye's mother celebrated the birth of her three sons with feasting and music, Ekwefi was the only person in the happy company who went about with a cloud on her brow. Her husband's wife took this for malevolence, as husbands' wives were wont to. How could she know that Ekwefi's bitterness did not flow outwards to others but inwards into her own soul; that she did not blame others for their good fortune but her own evil *chi* who denied her any?

At last Ezinma was born, and although ailing she seemed determined to live. At first Ekwefi accepted her, as she had accepted others – with listless resignation. But when she lived on to her fourth, fifth and sixth years, love returned once more to her mother, and, with love, anxiety. She determined to nurse her child to health, and she put all her being into it. She was rewarded by occasional spells of health during which Ezinma bubbled with energy like fresh palm-wine. At such times she seemed beyond danger. But all of a sudden she would go down again. Everybody knew she was an *ogbanje*. These sudden bouts of sickness and health were typical of her kind. But she had lived so long that perhaps she had decided to stay. Some of them did become tired of their evil rounds of birth and death, or took pity on their mothers, and stayed. Ekwefi believed deep inside her that Ezinma had come to stay. She believed because it was that faith alone that gave her own life any kind of meaning. And this faith had been strengthened when a year or so ago a medicine man had dug up Ezinma's *iyi-uwa*. Everyone knew then that she would live because her bond with the world of *ogbanje* had been broken. Ekwefi was reassured. But such was her anxiety for her daughter that she could not rid herself completely of her fear. And although she believed that the *iyi-uwa* which had been dug up was genuine, she could not ignore the fact that some really evil children sometimes misled people into digging up a specious one.

But Ezinma's *iyi-uwa* had looked real enough. It was

a smooth pebble wrapped in a dirty rag. The man who dug it up was the same Okagbue who was famous in all the clan for his knowledge in these matters. Ezinma had not wanted to cooperate with him at first. But that was only to be expected. No *ogbanje* would yield her secrets easily, and most of them never did because they died too young – before they could be asked questions.

'Where did you bury your *iyi-uwa*?' Okagbue had asked Ezinma. She was nine then and was just recovering from a serious illness.

'What is *iyi-uwa*?' she asked in return.

'You know what it is. You buried it in the ground somewhere so that you can die and return again to torment your mother.'

Ezinma looked at her mother, whose eyes, sad and pleading, were fixed on her.

'Answer the question at once,' roared Okonkwo, who stood beside her. All the family were there and some of the neighbors too.

'Leave her to me,' the medicine man told Okonkwo in a cool, confident voice. He turned again to Ezinma. 'Where did you bury your *iyi-uwa*?'

'Where they bury children,' she replied, and the quiet spectators murmured to themselves.

'Come along then and show me the spot,' said the medicine man.

The crowd set out with Ezinma leading the way and Okagbue following closely behind her. Okonkwo came next and Ekwefi followed him. When she came to the main road, Ezinma turned left as if she was going to the stream.

'But you said it was where they bury children?' asked the medicine man.

'No,' said Ezinma, whose feeling of importance was manifest in her sprightly walk. She sometimes broke

71

into a run and stopped again suddenly. The crowd
followed her silently. Women and children returning
from the stream with pots of water on their heads
wondered what was happening until they saw Okagbue and guessed that it must be something to do with
ogbanje. And they all knew Ekwefi and her daughter
very well.

When she got to the big udala tree Ezinma turned
left into the bush, and the crowd followed her. Because of her size she made her way through trees and
creepers more quickly than her followers. The bush
was alive with the tread of feet on dry leaves and sticks
and the moving aside of tree branches. Ezinma went
deeper and deeper and the crowd went with her.
Then she suddenly turned round and began to walk
back to the road. Everybody stood to let her pass and
then filed after her.

'If you bring us all this way for nothing I shall beat
sense into you,' Okonkwo threatened.

'I have told you to let her alone. I know how to deal
with them,' said Okagbue.

Ezinma led the way back to the road, looked left
and right and turned right. And so they arrived home
again.

'Where did you bury your *iyi-uwa*?' asked Okagbue
when Ezinma finally stopped outside her father's *obi*.
Okagbue's voice was unchanged. It was quiet and
confident.

'It is near that orange tree,' Ezinma said.

'And why did you not say so, you wicked daughter
of Akalogoli?' Okonkwo swore furiously. The medicine man ignored him.

'Come and show me the exact spot,' he said quietly
to Ezinma.

'It is here,' she said when they got to the tree.

'Point at the spot with your finger,' said Okagbue.

72

'It is here,' said Ezinma touching the ground with her finger. Okonkwo stood by, rumbling like thunder in the rainy season.

'Bring me a hoe,' said Okagbue.

When Ekwefi brought the hoe, he had already put aside his goatskin bag and his big cloth and was in his underwear, a long and thin strip of cloth wound round the waist like a belt and then passed between the legs to be fastened to the belt behind. He immediately set to work digging a pit where Ezinma had indicated. The neighbors sat around watching the pit becoming deeper and deeper. The dark top soil soon gave way to the bright red earth with which women scrubbed the floors and walls of huts. Okagbue worked tirelessly and in silence, his back shining with perspiration. Okonkwo stood by the pit. He asked Okagbue to come up and rest while he took a hand. But Okagbue said he was not tired yet.

Ekwefi went into her hut to cook yams. Her husband had brought out more yams than usual because the medicine man had to be fed. Ezinma went with her and helped in preparing the vegetables.

'There is too much green vegetable,' she said.

'Don't you see the pot is full of yams?' Ekwefi asked. 'And you know how leaves become smaller after cooking.'

'Yes,' said Ezinma, 'that was why the snake-lizard killed his mother.'

'Very true,' said Ekwefi.

'He gave his mother seven baskets of vegetables to cook and in the end there were only three. And so he killed her,' said Ezinma.

'That is not the end of the story.'

'Oho,' said Ezinma. 'I remember now. He brought another seven baskets and cooked them himself. And there were again only three. So he killed himself too.'

73

Outside the *obi* Okagbue and Okonkwo were digging the pit to find where Ezinma had buried her *iyi-uwa.* Neighbors sat around, watching. The pit was now so deep that they no longer saw the digger. They only saw the red earth he threw up mounting higher and higher. Okonkwo's son, Nwoye, stood near the edge of the pit because he wanted to take in all that happened.

Okagbue had again taken over the digging from Okonkwo. He worked, as usual, in silence. The neighbors and Okonkwo's wives were now talking. The children had lost interest and were playing.

Suddenly Okagbue sprang to the surface with the agility of a leopard.

'It is very near now,' he said. 'I have felt it.'

There was immediate excitement and those who were sitting jumped to their feet.

'Call your wife and child,' he said to Okonkwo. But Ekwefi and Ezinma had heard the noise and run out to see what it was.

Okagbue went back into the pit, which was now surrounded by spectators. After a few more hoe-fuls of earth he struck the *iyi-uwa.* He raised it carefully with the hoe and threw it to the surface. Some women ran away in fear when it was thrown. But they soon returned and everyone was gazing at the rag from a reasonable distance. Okagbue emerged and without saying a word or even looking at the spectators he went to his goatskin bag, took out two leaves and began to chew them. When he had swallowed them, he took up the rag with left hand and began to untie it. And then the smooth, shiny pebble fell out. He picked it up.

'Is this yours?' he asked Ezinma.

'Yes,' she replied. All the women shouted with joy because Ekwefi's troubles were at last ended.

All this had happened more than a year ago and

Ezinma had not been ill since. And then suddenly she had begun to shiver in the night. Ekwefi brought her to the fireplace, spread her mat on the floor and built a fire. But she had got worse and worse. As she knelt by her, feeling with her palm the wet, burning forehead, she prayed a thousand times. Although her husband's wives were saying that it was nothing more than *iba*, she did not hear them.

Okonkwo returned from the bush carrying on his left shoulder a large bundle of grasses and leaves, roots and barks of medicinal trees and shrubs. He went into Ekwefi's hut, put down his load and sat down.

'Get me a pot,' he said, 'and leave the child alone.'

Ekwefi went to bring the pot and Okonkwo selected the best from his bundle, in their due proportions, and cut them up. He put them in the pot and Ekwefi poured in some water.

'Is that enough?' she asked when she had poured in about half of the water in the bowl.

'A little more . . . I said *a little*. Are you deaf?' Okonkwo roared at her.

She set the pot on the fire and Okonkwo took up his machete to return to his *obi*.

'You must watch the pot carefully,' he said as he went, 'and don't allow it to boil over. If it does its power will be gone.' He went away to his hut and Ekwefi began to tend the medicine pot almost as if it was itself a sick child. Her eyes went constantly from Ezinma to the boiling pot and back to Ezinma.

Okonkwo returned when he felt the medicine had cooked long enough. He looked it over and said it was done.

'Bring me a low stool for Ezinma,' he said, 'and a thick mat.'

75

He took down the pot from the fire and placed it in front of the stool. He then roused Ezinma and placed her on the stool, astride the steaming pot. The thick mat was thrown over both. Ezinma struggled to escape from the choking and overpowering steam, but she was held down. She started to cry.

When the mat was at last removed she was drenched in perspiration. Ekwefi mopped her with a piece of cloth and she lay down on a dry mat and was soon asleep.

Ten

LARGE crowds began to gather on the village *ilo* as soon as the edge had worn off the sun's heat and it was no longer painful on the body. Most communal ceremonies took place at that time of the day, so that even when it was said that a ceremony would begin 'after the midday meal' everyone understood that it would begin a long time later, when the sun's heat had softened.

It was clear from the way the crowd stood or sat that the ceremony was for men. There were many women, but they looked on from the fringe like outsiders. The titled men and elders sat on their stools waiting for the trials to begin. In front of them was a row of stools on which nobody sat. There were nine of them. Two little groups of people stood at a respectable distance beyond the stools. They faced the elders. There were three men in one group and three men and one woman in the other. The woman was Mgbafo and the three men with her were her brothers. In the other group were her husband, Uzowulu, and his relatives. Mgbafo and her brothers were as still as statues into whose faces the artist has molded defiance. Uzowulu and his relatives, on the other hand, were whispering together. It looked like whispering, but they were really talking at the top of their voices. Everybody in the crowd was talking. It was like the market. From a distance the noise was a deep rumble carried by the wind.

An iron gong sounded, setting up a wave of expectation in the crowd. Everyone looked in the direction

77

of the *egwugwu* house. *Gome, gome, gome, gome* went the gong, and a powerful flute blew a high-pitched blast. Then came the voices of the *egwugwu*, gutteral and awesome. The wave struck the women and children and there was a backward stampede. But it was momentary. They were already far enough where they stood and there was room for running away if any of the *egwugwu* should go towards them.

The drum sounded again and the flute blew. The *egwugwu* house was now a pandemonium of quavering voices: *Aru oyim de de de dei!* filled the air as the spirits of the ancestors, just emerged from the earth, greeted themselves in their esoteric language. The *egwugwu* house into which they emerged faced the forest, away from the crowd, who saw only its back with the many colored patterns and drawings done by specially chosen women at regular intervals. These women never saw the inside of the hut. No woman ever did. They scrubbed and painted the outside walls under the supervision of men. If they imagined what was inside, they kept their imagination to themselves. No woman ever asked questions about the most powerful and the most secret cult in the clan.

Aru oyim de de de dei! flew around the dark, closed hut like tongues of fire. The ancestral spirits of the clan were abroad. The metal gong beat continuously now and the flute, shrill and powerful, floated on the chaos.

And then the *egwugwu* appeared. The women and children sent up a great shout and took to their heels. It was instinctive. A woman fled as soon as an *egwugwu* came in sight. And when, as on that day, nine of the greatest masked spirits in the clan came out together it was a terrifying spectacle. Even Mgbafo took to her heels and had to be restrained by her brothers.

Each of the nine *egwugwu* represented a village of

the clan. Their leader was called Evil Forest. Smoke poured out of his head.

The nine villages of Umuofia had grown out of the nine sons of the first father of the clan. Evil Forest represented the village of Umueru, or the children of Eru, who was the eldest of the nine sons.

'*Umuofia kwenu!*' shouted the leading *egwugwu*, pushing the air with his raffia arms. The elders of the clan replied, '*Yaa!*'

'*Umuofia kwenu!*'

'*Yaa!*'

'*Umuofia kwenu!*'

'*Yaa!*'

Evil Forest then thrust the pointed end of his rattling staff into the earth. And it began to shake and rattle, like something agitating with a metallic life. He took the first of the empty stools and the eight other *egwugwu* began to sit in order of seniority after him.

Okonkwo's wives, and perhaps other women as well, might have noticed that the second *egwugwu* had the springy walk of Okonkwo. And they might also have noticed that Okonkwo was not among the titled men and elders who sat behind the row of *egwugwu*. But if they thought these things they kept them within themselves. The *egwugwu* with the springy walk was one of the dead fathers of the clan. He looked terrible with the smoked raffia body, a huge wooden face painted white except for the round hollow eyes and the charred teeth that were as big as a man's fingers. On his head were two powerful horns.

When all the *egwugwu* had sat down and the sound of the many tiny bells and rattles on their bodies had subsided, Evil Forest addressed the two groups of people facing them.

'Uzowulu's body, I salute you,' he said. Spirits always addressed humans as 'bodies.' Uzowulu bent down and touched the earth with his right hand as a sign of submission.

'Our father, my hand has touched the ground,' he said.

'Uzowulu's body, do you know me?' asked the spirit.

'How can I know you, father? You are beyond our knowledge.'

Evil Forest then turned to the other group and addressed the eldest of the three brothers.

'The body of Odukwe, I greet you,' he said, and Odukwe bent down and touched the earth. The hearing then began.

Uzowulu stepped forward and presented his case.

'That woman standing there is my wife, Mgbafo. I married her with my money and my yams. I do not owe my in-laws anything. I owe them no yams. I owe them no coco-yams. One morning three of them came to my house, beat me up and took my wife and children away. This happened in the rainy season. I have waited in vain for my wife to return. At last I went to my in-laws and said to them, "You have taken back your sister. I did not send her away. You yourselves took her. The law of the clan is that you should return her bride-price." But my wife's brothers said they had nothing to tell me. So I have brought the matter to the fathers of the clan. My case is finished. I salute you.'

'Your words are good,' said the leader of the *egwugwu*. 'Let us hear Odukwe. His words may also be good.'

Odukwe was short and thickset. He stepped forward, saluted the spirits and began his story.

'My in-law has told you that we went to his house, beat him up and took our sister and her children away. All that is true. He told you that he came to take back her bride-price and we refused to give it him.

That also is true. My in-law, Uzowulu, is a beast. My sister lived with him for nine years. During those years no single day passed in the sky without his beating the woman. We have tried to settle their quarrels time without number and on each occasion Uzowulu was guilty –'

'It is a lie!' Uzowulu shouted.

'Two years ago,' continued Odukwe, 'when she was pregnant, he beat her until she miscarried.'

'It is a lie. She miscarried after she had gone to sleep with her lover.'

'Uzowulu's body, I salute you,' said Evil Forest, silencing him. 'What kind of lover sleeps with a pregnant woman?' There was a loud murmur of approbation from the crowd. Odukwe continued:

'Last year when my sister was recovering from an illness, he beat her again so that if the neighbors had not gone in to save her she would have been killed. We heard of it, and did as you have been told. The law of Umuofia is that if a woman runs away from her husband her bride-price is returned. But in this case she ran away to save her life. Her two children belong to Uzowulu. We do not dispute it, but they are too young to leave their mother. If, in the other hand, Uzowulu should recover from his madness and come in the proper way to beg his wife to return she will do so on the understanding that if he ever beats her again we shall cut off his genitals for him.'

The crowd roared with laughter. Evil Forest rose to his feet and order was immediately restored. A steady cloud of smoke rose from his head. He sat down again and called two witnesses. They were both Uzowulu's neighbors, and they agreed about the beating. Evil Forest then stood up, pulled out his staff and thrust it into the earth again. He ran a few steps in the

direction of the women; they all fled in terror, only to
return to their places almost immediately. The nine
egwugwu then went away to consult together in their
house. They were silent for a long time. Then the
metal gong sounded and the flute was blown. The
egwugwu had emerged once again from their underground home. They saluted one another and then
reappeared on the *ilo*.

'*Umuofia kwenu!*' roared Evil Forest, facing the
elders and grandees of the clan.

'*Yaa!*' replied the thunderous crowd; then silence
descended from the sky and swallowed the noise.

Evil Forest began to speak and all the while he
spoke everyone was silent. The eight other *egwugwu*
were as still as statues.

'We have heard both sides of the case,' said Evil
Forest. 'Our duty is not to blame this man or to praise
that, but to settle the dispute.' He turned to Uzowulu's group and allowed a short pause.

'Uzowulu's body, I salute you,' he said.

'Our father, my hand has touched the ground,'
replied Uzowulu, touching the earth.

'Uzowulu's body, do you know me?'

'How can I know you, father? You are beyond our
knowledge,' Uzowulu replied.

'I am Evil Forest. I kill a man on the day that his
life is sweetest to him.'

'That is true,' replied Uzowulu.

'Go to your in-laws with a pot of wine and beg your
wife to return to you. It is not bravery when a man
fights with a woman.' He turned to Odukwe, and
allowed a brief pause.

'Odukwe's body, I greet you,' he said.

'My hand is on the ground,' replied Odukwe.

'Do you know me?'

'No man can know you,' replied Odukwe.

'I am Evil Forest, I am Dry-meat-that-fills-the-mouth, I am Fire-that-burns-without-faggots. If your in-law brings wine to you, let your sister go with him. I salute you.' He pulled his staff from the hard earth and thrust it back.

'*Umuofia kwenu!*' he roared, and the crowd answered.

'I don't know why such a trifle should come before the *egwugwu*,' said one elder to another.

'Don't you know what kind of man Uzowulu is? He will not listen to any other decision,' replied the other.

As they spoke two other groups of people had replaced the first before the *egwugwu*, and a great land case began.

Eleven

THE night was impenetrably dark. The moon had been rising later and later every night until now it was seen only at dawn. And whenever the moon forsook evening and rose at cock-crow the nights were as black as charcoal.

Ezinma and her mother sat on a mat on the floor after their supper of yam foo-foo and bitter-leaf soup. A palm-oil lamp gave out yellowish light. Without it, it would have been impossible to eat; one could not have known where one's mouth was in the darkness of that night. There was an oil lamp in all the four huts on Okonkwo's compound, and each hut seen from the others looked like a soft eye of yellow half-light set in the solid massiveness of night.

The world was silent except for the shrill cry of insects, which was part of the night, and the sound of wooden mortar and pestle as Nwayieke pounded her foo-foo. Nwayieke lived four compounds away, and she was notorious for her late cooking. Every woman in the neighborhood knew the sound of Nwayieke's mortar and pestle. It was also part of the night.

Okonkwo had eaten from his wives' dishes and was now reclining with his back against the wall. He searched his bag and brought out his snuff-bottle. He turned it on to his left palm, but nothing came out. He hit the bottle against his knee to shake up the tobacco. That was always the trouble with Okeke's snuff. It very quickly went damp, and there was too much saltpeter in it. Okonkwo had not bought snuff from him for a long time. Idigo was the man who knew how to grind good snuff. But he had recently fallen ill.

Low voices, broken now and again by singing, reached Okonkwo from his wives' huts as each woman and her children told folk stories. Ekwefi and her daughter, Ezinma, sat on a mat on the floor. It was Ekwefi's turn to tell a story.

'Once upon a time,' she began, 'all the birds were invited to a feast in the sky. They were very happy and began to prepare themselves for the great day. They painted their bodies with red cam wood and drew beautiful patterns on them with *uli*.

'Tortoise saw all these preparations and soon discovered what it all meant. Nothing that happened in the world of the animals ever escaped his notice; he was full of cunning. As soon as he heard of the great feast in the sky his throat began to itch at the very thought. There was a famine in those days and Tortoise had not eaten a good meal for two moons. His body rattled like a piece of dry stick in his empty shell. So he began to plan how he would go to the sky.'

'But he had no wings,' said Ezinma.

'Be patient,' replied her mother. 'That is the story. Tortoise had no wings, but he went to the birds and asked to be allowed to go with them.

' "We know you too well," said the birds when they had heard him. "You are full of cunning and you are ungrateful. If we allow you to come with us you will soon begin your mischief."

' "You do not know me," said Tortoise. "I am a changed man. I have learned that a man who makes trouble for others is also making it for himself."

'Tortoise had a sweet tongue, and within a short time all the birds agreed that he was a changed man, and they each gave him a feather, with which he made two wings.

'At last the great day came and Tortoise was the first to arrive at the meeting place. When all the birds had gathered together, they set off in a body. Tortoise was very happy and voluble as he flew among the birds, and he was soon chosen as the man to speak for the party because he was a great orator.

' "There is one important thing which we must not forget," he said as they flew on their way. "When people are invited to a great feast like this, they take new names for the occasion. Our hosts in the sky will expect us to honor this age-old custom."

'None of the birds had heard of this custom but they knew that Tortoise, in spite of his failings in other directions, was a widely-traveled man who knew the customs of different peoples. And so they each took a new name. When they had all taken, Tortoise also took one. He was to be called *All of you.*

'At last the party arrived in the sky and their hosts were very happy to see them. Tortoise stood up in his many-colored plumage and thanked them for their invitation. His speech was so eloquent that all the birds were glad they had brought him, and nodded their heads in approval of all he said. Their hosts took him as the king of the birds, especially as he looked somewhat different from the others.

'After kola nuts had been presented and eaten, the people of the sky set before their guests the most delectable dishes Tortoise had ever seen or dreamed of. The soup was brought out hot from the fire and in the very pot in which it had been cooked. It was full of meat and fish. Tortoise began to sniff aloud. There was pounded yam and also yam pottage cooked with palm-oil and fresh fish. There were also pots of palm-wine. When everything had been set before the guests, one of the people of the sky came forward and tasted a little from each pot. He then invited the birds to eat. But Tortoise jumped to his feet and asked: "For whom have you prepared this feast?"

' "For all of you," replied the man.

'Tortoise turned to the birds and said: " You remember that my name is *All of you.* The custom here is to serve the spokesman first and the others later. They will serve you when I have eaten."

'He began to eat and the birds grumbled angrily. The people of the sky thought it must be their custom to leave all the food for their king. And so Tortoise ate the best part of the food and then drank two pots of palm-wine, so that he was full of food and drink and his body filled out in his shell.

'The birds gathered round to eat what was left and to peck at the bones he had thrown all about the floor. Some of them were too angry to eat. They chose to fly home on an empty stomach. But before they left each took back the feather he had lent to Tortoise. And there he stood in his hard shell full of food and wine but without any wings to fly home. He asked the birds to take a message for his wife, but they all refused. In the end Parrot, who had felt more angry than the others, suddenly changed his mind and agreed to take the message.

' "Tell my wife," said Tortoise, "to bring out all the soft things in my house and cover the compound with them so that I can jump down from the sky without very great danger."

'Parrot promised to deliver the message, and then flew away. But when he reached Tortoise's house he told his wife to bring out all the hard things in the house. And so she brought out her husband's hoes, machetes, spears, guns and even his cannon. Tortoise looked down from the sky and saw his wife bringing things out, but it was too far to see what they were. When all seemed ready he let himself go. He fell and fell and fell until he began to fear that he would never stop falling. And then like the sound of his cannon he crashed on the compound.'

'Did he die?' asked Ezinma.

'No,' replied Ekwefi. 'His shell broke into pieces. But there was a great medicine man in the neighborhood. Tortoise's wife sent for him and he gathered all the bits of shell and stuck them together. That is why Tortoise's shell is not smooth.'

'There is no song in the story,' Ezinma pointed out.

'No,' said Ekwefi. 'I shall think of another one with a song. But it is your turn now.'

'Once upon a time,' Ezinma began, 'Tortoise and Cat went to wrestle against Yams – no, that is not the beginning. Once upon a time there was a great famine in the land of animals. Everybody was lean except Cat, who was fat and whose body shone as if oil was rubbed on it . . .'

She broke off because at that very moment a loud and high-pitched voice broke the outer silence of the night. It was Chielo, the priestess of Agbala, prophesying. There was nothing new in that. Once in a while Chielo was possessed by the spirit of her god and she began to prophesy. But tonight she was addressing her prophecy and greetings to Okonkwo, and so everyone in his family listened. The folk stories stopped.

'*Agbala do-o-o-o! Agbala ekeneo-o-o-o,*' came the voice like a sharp knife cutting through the night. '*Okonkwo! Agbala ekene gio-o-o-o! Agbala cholu ifu ada ya Ezinmao-o-o-o!*'

At the mention of Ezinma's name Ekwefi jerked her head sharply like an animal that had sniffed death in the air. Her heart jumped painfully within her.

The priestess had now reached Okonkwo's compound and was talking with him outside his hut. She was saying again and again that Agbala wanted to see his daughter, Ezinma. Okonkwo pleaded with her to come back in the morning because Ezinma was now asleep. But Chielo ignored what he was trying to say and went on shouting that Agbala wanted to see his daughter. Her voice was as clear as metal, and Okonkwo's women and children heard from their huts all that she said. Okonkwo was still pleading that the girl had been ill of late and was asleep. Ekwefi quickly took her to their bedroom and placed her on their high bamboo bed.

The priestess screamed. 'Beware, Okonkwo!' she warned. 'Beware of exchanging words with Agbala. Does a man speak when a god speaks? Beware!'

She walked through Okonkwo's hut into the circular compound and went straight toward Ekwefi's hut. Okonkwo came after her.

'Ekwefi,' she called, 'Agbala greets you. Where is my daughter, Ezinma? Agbala wants to see her.'

Ekwefi came out from her hut carrying her oil lamp in her left hand. There was a light wind blowing, so she cupped her right hand to shelter the flame. Nwoye's mother, also carrying an oil lamp, emerged from her hut. The children stood in the darkness outside their hut watching the strange event. Okonkwo's youngest wife also came out and joined the others.

'Where does Agbala want to see her?' Ekwefi asked.

'Where else but in his house in the hills and the caves?' replied the priestess.

'I will come with you, too,' Ekwefi said firmly.

'*Tufia-a!*' the priestess cursed, her voice cracking like the angry bark of thunder in the dry season. 'How dare you, woman, to go before the mighty Agbala of your own accord? Beware, woman, lest he strike you in his anger. Bring me my daughter.'

Ekwefi went into her hut and came out again with Ezinma.

'Come, my daughter,' said the priestess. 'I shall carry you on my back. A baby on its mother's back does not know that the way is long.'

Ezinma began to cry. She was used to Chielo calling her 'my daughter.' But it was a different Chielo she now saw in the yellow half-light.

'Don't cry, my daughter,' said the priestess, 'lest Agbala be angry with you.'

'Don't cry,' said Ekwefi, 'she will bring you back very soon. I shall give you some fish to eat.' She went into the hut again and brought down the smoke-black basket in which she kept her dried fish and other ingredients for cooking soup. She broke a piece in two and gave it to Ezinma, who clung to her.

'Don't be afraid,' said Ekwefi, stroking her head, which was shaved in places, leaving a regular pattern of hair. They went outside again. The priestess bent down on one knee and Ezinma climbed on her back, her left palm closed on her fish and her eyes gleaming with tears.

'*Agbala do-o-o-o! Agbala ekeneo-o-o-o!* . . .' Chielo began once again to chant greetings to her god. She turned round sharply and walked through Okonkwo's hut, bending very low at the eaves. Ezinma was crying loudly now, calling on her mother. The two voices disappeared into the thick darkness.

A strange and sudden weakness descended on Ekwefi as she stood gazing in the direction of the voices like a hen whose only chick has been carried away by a kite. Ezinma's voice soon faded away and only Chielo was heard moving farther and farther into the distance.

'Why do you stand there as though she had been kidnapped?' asked Okonkwo as he went back to his hut.

'She will bring her back soon,' Nwoye's mother said.

But Ekwefi did not hear these consolations. She stood for a while, and then, all of a sudden, made up her mind. She hurried through Okonkwo's hut and went outside. 'Where are you going?' he asked.

'I am following Chielo,' she replied and disappeared in the darkness. Okonkwo cleared his throat, and brought out his snuff-bottle from the goatskin bag by his side.

The priestess' voice was already growing faint in the distance. Ekwefi hurried to the main footpath and turned left in the direction of the voice. Her eyes were useless to her in the darkness. But she picked her way easily on the sandy footpath hedged on either side by branches and damp leaves. She began to run, holding her breasts with her hands to stop them flapping noisily against her body. She hit her left foot against an outcropped root, and terror seized her. It was an ill omen. She ran faster. But Chielo's voice was still a long way away. Had she been running too? How could she go so fast with Ezinma on her back? Although the night was cool, Ekwefi was beginning to feel hot from her running. She continually ran into the luxuriant weeds and creepers that walled in the path. Once she tripped up and fell. Only then did she realize, with a start, that Chielo had stopped her chanting. Her heart beat violently and she stood still. Then Chielo's renewed outburst came from only a few paces ahead. But Ekwefi could not see her. She shut her eyes for a while and opened them again in an effort to see. But it was useless. She could not see beyond her nose.

There were no stars in the sky because there was a rain-cloud. Fireflies went about with their tiny green lamps, which only made the darkness more profound. Between Chielo's outbursts the night was alive with the shrill tremor of forest insects woven into the darkness.

'*Agbala do-o-o-o!* . . . *Agbala ekeneo-o-o-o!* . . .' Ekwefi trudged behind, neither getting too near nor keeping too far back. She thought they must be going towards the sacred cave. Now that she walked slowly she had time to think. What would she do when they got to the cave? She would not dare to enter. She would wait at the mouth, all alone in that fearful place. She thought of all the terrors of the night. She remembered that night, long ago, when she had seen *Ogbu-agali-odu*, one of those evil essences loosed upon the world by the potent 'medicines' which the tribe had made in the distant past against its enemies but had now forgotten how to control. Ekwefi had been returning from the stream with her mother on a dark night like this when they saw its glow as it flew in their direction. They had thrown down their water-pots and lain by the roadside expecting the sinister light to descend on them and kill them. That was the only time Ekwefi ever saw *Ogbu-agali-odu*. But although it had happened so long ago, her blood still ran cold whenever she remembered that night.

The priestess' voice came at longer intervals now, but its vigor was undiminished. The air was cool and damp with dew. Ezinma sneezed. Ekwefi muttered, 'Life to you.' At the same time the priestess also said, 'Life to you, my daughter.' Ezinma's voice from the darkness warmed her mother's heart. She trudged slowly along.

And then the priestess screamed. 'Somebody is walking behind me!' she said. 'Whether you are spirit or man, may Agbala shave your head with a blunt razor! May he twist your neck until you see your heels!'

Ekwefi stood rooted to the spot. One mind said to her: 'Woman, go home before Agbala does you harm.' But she could not. She stood until Chielo had increased the distance between them and she began to follow again. She had already walked so long that she began to feel a slight numbness in the limbs and in the head. Then it occurred to her that they could not have been heading for the cave. They must have by-passed it long ago; they must be going towards Umuachi, the farthest village in the clan. Chielo's voice now came after long intervals.

It seemed to Ekwefi that the night had become a little lighter. The cloud had lifted and a few stars were out. The moon must be preparing to rise, its sullenness over. When the moon rose late in the night, people said it was refusing food, as a sullen husband refuses his wife's food when they have quarreled.

'*Agbala do-o-o-o! Umuachi! Agbala ekene unuo-o-o!*' It was just as Ekwefi had thought. The priestess was now saluting the village of Umuachi. It was unbelievable, the distance they had covered. As they emerged into the open village from the narrow forest track the darkness was softened and it became possible to see the vague shape of trees. Ekwefi screwed her eyes up in an effort to see her daughter and the priestess, but whenever she thought she saw their shape it immediately dissolved like a melting lump of darkness. She walked numbly along.

Chielo's voice was now rising continuously, as when she first set out. Ekwefi had a feeling of spacious openness, and she guessed they must be on the village *ilo,* or playground. And she realized too with something like a jerk that Chielo was no longer moving forward. She was, in fact, returning. Ekwefi quickly moved away from her line of retreat. Chielo passed by, and they began to go back the way they had come.

It was a long and weary journey and Ekwefi felt like a sleepwalker most of the way. The moon was definitely rising, and although it had not yet appeared on the sky its light had already melted down the darkness. Ekwefi could now discern the figure of the priestess and her burden. She slowed down her pace so as to increase the distance between them. She was afraid of what might happen if Chielo suddenly turned round and saw her.

She had prayed for the moon to rise. But now she found the half-light of the incipient moon more terrifying than darkness. The world was now peopled with vague, fantastic figures that dissolved under her steady gaze and then formed again in new shapes. At one stage Ekwefi was so afraid that she nearly called out to Chielo for companionship and human sympathy. What she had seen was the shape of a man climbing a palm tree, his head pointing to the earth and his legs skywards. But at that very moment Chielo's voice rose again in her possessed chanting, and Ekwefi recoiled, because there was no humanity there. It was not the same Chielo who sat with her in the market and sometimes bought beancakes for Ezinma, whom she called her daughter. It was a different woman – the priestess of Agbala, the Oracle of the Hills and Caves. Ekwefi trudged along between two fears. The sound of her benumbed steps seemed to come from some other person walking behind her. Her arms were folded across her bare breasts. Dew fell heavily and the air was cold. She could no longer think, not even about the terrors of night. She just jogged along in a half-sleep, only waking to full life when Chielo sang.

At last they took a turning and began to head for the caves. From then on, Chielo never ceased in her chanting. She greeted her god in a multitude of names – the owner of the future, the messenger of earth, the god who cut a man down when his life was sweetest to him. Ekwefi was also awakened and her benumbed fears revived.

The moon was now up and she could see Chielo and Ezinma clearly. How a woman could carry a child of that size so easily and for so long was a miracle. But Ekwefi was not thinking about that. Chielo was not a woman that night.

'*Agbala do-o-o-o! Agbala ekeneo-o-o! Chi negbu madu ubosi ndu ya nato ya uto daluo-o-o! . . .*'

Ekwefi could already see the hills looming in the moonlight. They formed a circular ring with a break at one point through which the foot-track led to the center of the circle.

As soon as the priestess stepped into this ring of hills her voice was not only doubled in strength but was thrown back on all sides. It was indeed the shrine of a great god. Ekwefi picked her way carefully and quietly. She was already beginning to doubt the wisdom of her coming. Nothing would happen to Ezinma, she thought. And if anything happened to her could she stop it? She would not dare to enter the underground caves. Her coming was quite useless, she thought.

As these things went through her mind she did not realize how close they were to the cave mouth. And so when the priestess with Ezinma on her back disappeared through a hole hardly big enough to pass a hen, Ekwefi broke into a run as though to stop them. As she stood gazing at the circular darkness which had swallowed them, tears gushed from her eyes, and she swore within her that if she heard Ezinma cry she would rush into the cave to defend her against all the gods in the world. She would die with her.

Having sworn that oath, she sat down on a stony ledge and waited. Her fear had vanished. She could hear the priestess' voice, all its metal taken out of it by the vast emptiness of the cave. She buried her face in her lap and waited.

She did not know how long she waited. It must have been a very long time. Her back was turned on the footpath that led out of the hills. She must have heard a noise behind her and turned round sharply. A man stood there with a machete in his hand. Ekwefi uttered a scream and sprang to her feet.

'Don't be foolish,' said Okonkwo's voice. 'I thought you were going into the shrine with Chielo,' he mocked.

Ekwefi did not answer. Tears of gratitude filled her eyes. She knew her daughter was safe.

'Go home and sleep,' said Okonkwo. 'I shall wait here.'

'I shall wait too. It is almost dawn. The first cock has crowed.'

As they stood there together, Ekwefi's mind went back to the days when they were young. She had married Anene because Okonkwo was too poor then to marry. Two years after her marriage to Anene she could bear it no longer and she ran away to Okonkwo. It had been early in the morning. The moon was shining. She was going to the stream to fetch water. Okonkwo's house was on the way to the stream. She went in and knocked at his door and he came out. Even in those days he was not a man of many words. He just carried her into his bed and in the darkness began to feel around her waist for the loose end of her cloth.

Twelve

ON the following morning the entire neighborhood wore a festive air because Okonkwo's friend, Obierika, was celebrating his daughter's *uri*. It was the day on which her suitor (having already paid the greater part of her bride-price) would bring palm-wine not only to her parents and immediate relatives but to the wide and extensive group of kinsmen called *umunna*. Everybody had been invited – men, women and children. But it was really a woman's ceremony and the central figures were the bride and her mother.

As soon as day broke, breakfast was hastily eaten and women and children began to gather at Obierika's compound to help the bride's mother in her difficult but happy task of cooking for a whole village.

Okonkwo's family was astir like any other family in the neighborhood. Nwoye's mother and Okonkwo's youngest wife were ready to set out for Obierika's compound with all their children. Nwoye's mother carried a basket of coco-yams, a cake of salt and smoked fish which she would present to Obierika's wife. Okonkwo's youngest wife, Ojiugo, also had a basket of plantains and coco-yams and a small pot of palm-oil. Their children carried pots of water.

Ekwefi was tired and sleepy from the exhausting experiences of the previous night. It was not very long since they had returned. The priestess, with Ezinma sleeping on her back, had crawled out of the shrine on her belly like a snake. She had not as much as

CHINUA ACHEBE

looked at Okonkwo and Ekwefi or shown any surprise at finding them at the mouth of the cave. She looked straight ahead of her and walked back to the village. Okonkwo and his wife followed at a respectful distance. They thought the priestess might be going to her house, but she went to Okonkwo's compound, passed through his *obi* and into Ekwefi's hut and walked into her bedroom. She placed Ezinma carefully on the bed and went away without saying a word to anybody.

Ezinma was still sleeping when everyone else was astir, and Ekwefi asked Nwoye's mother and Ojiugo to explain to Obierika's wife that she would be late. She had got ready her basket of coco-yams and fish, but she must wait for Ezinma to wake.

'You need some sleep yourself,' said Nwoye's mother. 'You look very tired.'

As they spoke Ezinma emerged from the hut, rubbing her eyes and stretching her spare frame. She saw the other children with their water-pots and remembered that they were going to fetch water for Obierika's wife. She went back to the hut and brought her pot.

'Have you slept enough?' asked her mother.

'Yes,' she replied. 'Let us go.'

'Not before you have had your breakfast,' said Ekwefi. And she went into her hut to warm the vegetable soup she had cooked last night.

'We shall be going,' said Nwoye's mother. 'I will tell Obierika's wife that you are coming later.' And so they all went to help Obierika's wife – Nwoye's mother with her four children and Ojiugo with her two.

As they trooped through Okonkwo's *obi* he asked: 'Who will prepare my afternoon meal?'

'I shall return to do it,' said Ojiugo.

Okonkwo was also feeling tired, and sleepy, for

although nobody else knew it, he had not slept at all last night. He had felt very anxious but did not show it. When Ekwefi had followed the priestess, he had allowed what he regarded as a reasonable and manly interval to pass and then gone with his machete to the shrine, where he thought they must be. It was only when he had got there that it had occurred to him that the priestess might have chosen to go round the villages first. Okonkwo had returned home and sat waiting. When he thought he had waited long enough he again returned to the shrine. But the Hills and the Caves were as silent as death. It was only on his fourth trip that he had found Ekwefi, and by then he had become gravely worried.

Obierika's compound was as busy as an anthill. Temporary cooking tripods were erected on every available space by bringing together three blocks of sun-dried earth and making a fire in their midst. Cooking pots went up and down the tripods, and foo-foo was pounded in a hundred wooden mortars. Some of the women cooked the yams and the cassava, and others prepared vegetable soup. Young men pounded the foo-foo or split firewood. The children made endless trips to the stream.

Three young men helped Obierika to slaughter the two goats with which the soup was made. They were very fat goats, but the fattest of all was tethered to a peg near the wall of the compound. It was as big as a small cow. Obierika had sent one of his relatives all the way to Umuike to buy that goat. It was the one he would present alive to his in-laws.

'The market of Umuike is a wonderful place,' said the young man who had been sent by Obierika to buy the giant goat. 'There are so many people on it that if you threw up a grain of sand it would not find a way to fall to earth again.'

'It is the result of a great medicine,' said Obierika. 'The people of Umuike wanted their market to grow and swallow up the markets of their neighbors. So they made a powerful medicine. Every market day, before the first cock-crow, this medicine stands on the market ground in the shape of an old woman with a fan. With this magic fan she beckons to the market all the neighboring clans. She beckons in front of her and behind her, to her right and to her left.'

'And so everybody comes,' said another man, 'honest men and thieves. They can steal your cloth from off your waist in that market.'

'Yes,' said Obierika. 'I wanted Nwankwo to keep a sharp eye and a sharp ear. There was once a man who went to sell a goat. He led it on a thick rope which he tied round his wrist. But as he walked through the market he realized that people were pointing at him as they do to a madman. He could not understand it until he looked back and saw that what he led at the end of the tether was not a goat but a heavy log of wood.'

'Do you think a thief can do that kind of thing single-handed?' asked Nwankwo.

'No,' said Obierika. 'They use medicine.'

When they had cut the goats' throats and collected the blood in a bowl, they held them over an open fire to burn off the hair, and the smell of burning hair blended with the smell of cooking. Then they washed them and cut them up for the women who prepared the soup.

All this anthill activity was going smoothly when a sudden interruption came. It was a cry in the distance: *Oji odu achu ijiji-o-o! (The one that uses its tail to drive flies away!)* Every woman immediately abandoned whatever she was doing and rushed out in the direction of the cry.

'We cannot all rush out like that, leaving what we are cooking to burn in the fire,' shouted Chielo, the priestess. 'Three or four of us should stay behind.'

'It is true,' said another woman. 'We will allow three or four women to stay behind.'

Five women stayed behind to look after the cooking-pots, and all the rest rushed away to see the cow that had been let loose. When they saw it they drove it back to its owner, who at once paid the heavy fine which the village imposed on anyone whose cow was let loose on his neighbors' crops. When the women had exacted the penalty they checked among themselves to see if any woman had failed to come out when the cry had been raised.

'Where is Mgbogo?' asked one of them.

'She is ill in bed,' said Mgbogo's next-door neighbor. 'She has *iba*.'

'The only other person is Udenkwo,' said another woman, 'and her child is not twenty-eight days yet.'

Those women whom Obierika's wife had not asked to help her with the cooking returned to their homes, and the rest went back, in a body, to Obierika's compound.

'Whose cow was it?' asked the women who had been allowed to stay behind.

'It was my husband's,' said Ezelagbo. 'One of the young children had opened the gate of the cow-shed.'

Early in the afternoon the first two pots of palm-wine arrived from Obierika's in-laws. They were duly presented to the women, who drank a cup or two each, to help them in their cooking. Some of it also went to the bride and her attendant maidens, who were putting the last delicate touches of razor to her coiffure and cam wood on her smooth skin.

When the heat of the sun began to soften, Obierika's son, Maduka, took a long broom and swept the ground in front of his father's *obi*. And as if they had been waiting for that, Obierika's relatives and friends began to arrive, every man with his goatskin bag hung on one shoulder and a rolled goatskin mat under his arm. Some of them were accompanied by their sons bearing carved wooden stools. Okonkwo was one of them. They sat in a half-circle and began to talk of many things. It would not be long before the suitors came.

Okonkwo brought out his snuff-bottle and offered it to Ogbuefi Ezenwa, who sat next to him. Ezenwa took it, tapped it on his knee-cap, rubbed his left palm on his body to dry it before tipping a little snuff into it. His actions were deliberate, and he spoke as he performed them:

'I hope our in-laws will bring many pots of wine. Although they come from a village that is known for being closefisted, they ought to know that Akueke is the bride for a king.'

'They dare not bring fewer than thirty pots,' said Okonkwo. 'I shall tell them my mind if they do.'

At that moment Obierika's son, Maduka, led out the giant goat from the inner compound, for his father's relatives to see. They all admired it and said that that was the way things should be done. The goat was then led back to the inner compound.

Very soon after, the in-laws began to arrive. Young men and boys in single file, each carrying a pot of wine, came first. Obierika's relatives counted the pots as they came. Twenty, twenty-five. There was a long break, and the hosts looked at each other as if to say, 'I told you.' Then more pots came. Thirty, thirty-five, forty, forty-five. The hosts nodded in approval and seemed to say, 'Now they are behaving like men.' Altogether there were fifty pots of wine. After the pot-bearers came Ibe, the suitor, and the elders of his family. They sat in a half-moon, thus completing a circle with their hosts. The pots of wine stood in their midst. Then the bride, her mother and a half a dozen other women and girls emerged from the inner compound, and went round the circle shaking hands with all. The bride's mother led the way, followed by the bride and the other women. The married women wore their best cloths and the girls wore red and black waist-beads and anklets of brass.

When the women retired, Obierika presented kola nuts to his in-laws. His eldest brother broke the first one. 'Life to all of us,' he said as he broke it. 'And let there be friendship between your family and ours.'

The crowd answered: '*Ee-e-e!*'

'We are giving you our daughter today. She will be a good wife to you. She will bear you nine sons like the mother of our town.'

'*Ee-e-e!*'

The oldest man in the camp of the visitors replied: 'It will be good for you and it will be good for us.'

'*Ee-e-e!*'

'This is not the first time my people have come to marry your daughter. My mother was one of you.'

'*Ee-e-e!*'

'And this will not be the last, because you understand us and we understand you. You are a great family.'

'*Ee-e-e!*'

'Prosperous men and great warriors.' He looked in the direction of Okonkwo. 'Your daughter will bear us sons like you.'

'*Ee-e-e!*'

The kola was eaten and the drinking of palm-wine began. Groups of four or five men sat round with a pot in their midst. As the evening wore on, food was presented to the guests. There were huge bowls of foo-foo and steaming pots of soup. There were also pots of yam pottage. It was a great feast.

As night fell, burning torches were set on wooden tripods and the young men raised a song. The elders sat in a big circle and the singers went round singing each man's praise as they came before him. They had something to say for every man. Some were great farmers, some were orators who spoke for the clan; Okonkwo was the greatest wrestler and warrior alive. When they had gone round the circle they settled down in the center, and girls came from the inner compound to dance. At first the bride was not among them. But when she finally appeared holding a cock in her right hand, a loud cheer rose from the crowd. All the other dancers made way for her. She presented the cock to the musicians and began to dance. Her brass anklets rattled as she danced and her body gleamed with cam wood in the soft yellow light. The musicians with their wood, clay and metal instruments went from song to song. And they were all gay. They sang the latest song in the village:

> 'If I hold her hand
>   She says, "Don't touch!"
> If I hold her foot
>   She says, "Don't touch!"
> But when I hold her waist-beads
>   She pretends not to know.'

The night was already far spent when the guests rose to go, taking their bride home to spend seven market weeks with her suitor's family. They sang songs as they went, and on their way they paid short courtesy visits to prominent men like Okonkwo, before they finally left for their village. Okonkwo made a present of two cocks to them.

Thirteen

GO-DI-DI-GO-GO-DI-GO. Di-go-go-di-go. It was the *ekwe* talking to the clan. One of the things every man learned was the language of the hollowed-out wooden instrument. Diim! Diim! Diim! boomed the cannon at intervals.

The first cock had not crowed, and Umuofia was still swallowed up in sleep and silence when the *ekwe* began to talk, and the cannon shattered the silence. Men stirred on their bamboo beds and listened anxiously. Somebody was dead. The cannon seemed to rend the sky. Di-go-go-di-go-di-di-go-go floated in the message-laden night air. The faint and distant wailing of women settled like a sediment of sorrow on the earth. Now and again a full-chested lamentation rose above the wailing whenever a man came into the place of death. He raised his voice once or twice in manly sorrow and then sat down with the other men listening to the endless wailing of the women and the esoteric language of the *ekwe*. Now and again the cannon boomed. The wailing of the women would not be heard beyond the village, but the *ekwe* carried the news to all the nine villages and even beyond. It began by naming the clan: *Umuofia obodo dike*, 'the land of the brave.' *Umuofia obodo dike! Umuofia obodo dike!* It said this over and over again, and as it dwelt on it, anxiety mounted in every heart that heaved on a bamboo bed that night. Then it went nearer and named the village: *Iguedo of the yellow grinding-stone!*' It was Okonkwo's village. Again and again

Iguedo was called and men waited breathlessly in all the nine villages. At last the man was named and people sighed 'E-u-u, Ezeudu is dead.' A cold shiver ran down Okonkwo's back as he remembered the last time the old man had visited him. 'That boy calls you father,' he had said. 'Bear no hand in his death.'

Ezeudu was a great man, and so all the clan was at his funeral. The ancient drums of death beat, guns and cannon were fired, and men dashed about in frenzy, cutting down every tree or animal they saw, jumping over walls and dancing on the roof. It was a warrior's funeral, and from morning till night warriors came and went in their age groups. They all wore smoked raffia skirts and their bodies were painted with chalk and charcoal. Now and again an ancestral spirit or *egwugwu* appeared from the underworld, speaking in a tremulous, unearthly voice and completely covered in raffia. Some of them were very violent, and there had been a mad rush for shelter earlier in the day when one appeared with a sharp machete and was only prevented from doing serious harm by two men who restrained him with the help of a strong rope tied round his waist. Sometimes he turned round and chased those men, and they ran for their lives. But they always returned to the long rope he trailed behind. He sang, in a terrifying voice, that Ekwensu, or Evil Spirit, had entered his eye.

But the most dreaded of all was yet to come. He was always alone and was shaped like a coffin. A sickly odor hung in the air wherever he went, and flies went with him. Even the greatest medicine men took shelter when he was near. Many years ago another *egwugwu* had dared to stand his ground before him and had been transfixed to the spot for two days. This one had only one hand and it carried a basket full of water.

But some of the *egwugwu* were quite harmless. One of them was so old and infirm that he leaned heavily on a stick. He walked unsteadily to the place where the corpse was laid, gazed at it a while and went away again – to the underworld.

The land of the living was not far removed from the domain of the ancestors. There was coming and going between them, especially at festivals and also when an old man died, because an old man was very close to the ancestors. A man's life from birth to death was a series of transition rites which brought him nearer and nearer to his ancestors.

Ezeudu had been the oldest man in his village, and at his death there were only three men in the whole clan who were older, and four or five others in his own age group. Whenever one of these ancient men appeared in the crowd to dance unsteadily the funeral steps of the tribe, younger men gave way and the tumult subsided.

It was a great funeral, such as befitted a noble warrior. As the evening drew near, the shouting and the firing of guns, the beating of drums and the brandishing and clanging of machetes increased.

Ezeudu had taken three titles in his life. It was a rare achievement. There were only four titles in the clan, and only one or two men in any generation ever achieved the fourth and highest. When they did, they became the lords of the land. Because he had taken titles, Ezeudu was to be buried after dark with only a glowing brand to light the sacred ceremony.

But before this quiet and final rite, the tumult increased tenfold. Drums beat violently and men leaped

THINGS FALL APART

up and down in frenzy. Guns were fired on all sides
and sparks flew out as machetes clanged together
in warriors' salutes. The air was full of dust and the
smell of gunpowder. It was then that the one-handed
spirit came, carrying a basket full of water. People
made way for him on all sides and the noise subsided.
Even the smell of gunpowder was swallowed in the
sickly smell that now filled the air. He danced a few
steps to the funeral drums and then went to see the
corpse.

'Ezeudu!' he called in his guttural voice. 'If you had
been poor in your last life I would have asked you to
be rich when you come again. But you were rich. If
you had been a coward, I would have asked you to
bring courage. But you were a fearless warrior. If you
had died young, I would have asked you to get life.
But you lived long. So I shall ask you to come again
the way you came before. If your death was the death
of nature, go in peace. But if a man caused it, do not
allow him a moment's rest.' He danced a few more
steps and went away.

The drums and the dancing began again and
reached fever-heat. Darkness was around the corner,
and the burial was near. Guns fired the last salute and
the cannon rent the sky. And then from the center of
the delirious fury came a cry of agony and shouts of
horror. It was as if a spell had been cast. All was silent.
In the center of the crowd a boy lay in a pool of blood.
It was the dead man's sixteen-year-old son, who with
his brothers and half-brothers had been dancing the
traditional farewell to their father. Okonkwo's gun
had exploded and a piece of iron had pierced the
boy's heart.

The confusion that followed was without parallel in
the tradition of Umuofia. Violent deaths were frequent, but nothing like this had ever happened.

109

The only course open to Okonkwo was to flee from the clan. It was a crime against the earth goddess to kill a clansman, and a man who committed it must flee from the land. The crime was of two kinds, male and female. Okonkwo had committed the female, because it had been inadvertent. He could return to the clan after seven years.

That night he collected his most valuable belongings into head-loads. His wives wept bitterly and their children wept with them without knowing why. Obierika and half a dozen other friends came to help and to console him. They each made nine or ten trips carrying Okonkwo's yams to store in Obierika's barn. And before the cock crowed Okonkwo and his family were fleeing to his motherland. It was a little village called Mbanta, just beyond the borders of Mbaino.

As soon as the day broke, a large crowd of men from Ezeudu's quarter stormed Okonkwo's compound, dressed in garbs of war. They set fire to his houses, demolished his red walls, killed his animals and destroyed his barn. It was the justice of the earth goddess, and they were merely her messengers. They had no hatred in their hearts against Okonkwo. His greatest friend, Obierika, was among them. They were merely cleansing the land which Okonkwo had polluted with the blood of a clansman.

Obierika was a man who thought about things. When the will of the goddess had been done, he sat down in his *obi* and mourned his friend's calamity. Why should a man suffer so grievously for an offense he had committed inadvertently? But although he thought for a long time he found no answer. He was merely led into greater complexities. He remembered his wife's twin children, whom he had thrown away.

What crime had they committed? The Earth had decreed that they were an offense on the land and must be destroyed. And if the clan did not exact punishment for an offense against the great goddess, her wrath was loosed on all the land and not just on the offender. As the elders said, if one finger brought oil it soiled the others.

PART TWO

Fourteen

OKONKWO was well received by his mother's kinsmen in Mbanta. The old man who received him was his mother's younger brother, who was now the eldest surviving member of that family. His name was Uchendu, and it was he who had received Okonkwo's mother twenty and ten years before when she had been brought home from Umuofia to be buried with her people. Okonkwo was only a boy then and Uchendu still remembered him crying the traditional farewell: 'Mother, mother, mother is going.'

That was many years ago. Today Okonkwo was not bringing his mother home to be buried with her people. He was taking his family of three wives and their children to seek refuge in his motherland. As soon as Uchendu saw him with his sad and weary company he guessed what had happened, and asked no questions. It was not until the following day that Okonkwo told him the full story. The old man listened silently to the end and then said with some relief: 'It is a female *ochu*.' And he arranged the requisite rites and sacrifices.

Okonkwo was given a plot of ground on which to build his compound, and two or three pieces of land on which to farm during the coming planting season. With the help of his mother's kinsmen he built himself an *obi* and three huts for his wives. He then installed his personal god and the symbols of his departed fathers. Each of Uchendu's five sons contributed three hundred seed-yams to enable their cousin to plant a farm, for as soon as the first rain came farming would begin.

At last the rain came. It was sudden and tremendous. For two or three moons the sun had been gathering strength till it seemed to breathe a breath of fire on the earth. All the grass had long been scorched brown, and the sands felt like live coals to the feet. Evergreen trees wore a dusty coat of brown. The birds were silenced in the forests, and the world lay panting under the live, vibrating heat. And then came the clap of thunder. It was an angry, metallic and thirsty clap, unlike the deep and liquid rumbling of the rainy season. A mighty wind arose and filled the air with dust. Palm trees swayed as the wind combed their leaves into flying crests like strange and fantastic coiffure.

When the rain finally came, it was in large, solid drops of frozen water which the people called 'the nuts of the water of heaven.' They were hard and painful on the body as they fell, yet young people ran about happily picking up the cold nuts and throwing them into their mouths to melt.

The earth quickly came to life and the birds in the forests fluttered around and chirped merrily. A vague scent of life and green vegetation was diffused in the air. As the rain began to fall more soberly and in smaller liquid drops, children sought for shelter, and all were happy, refreshed and thankful.

Okonkwo and his family worked very hard to plant a new farm. But it was like beginning life anew without the vigor and enthusiasm of youth, like learning to become left-handed in old age. Work no longer had for him the pleasure it used to have, and when there was no work to do he sat in a silent half-sleep.

His life had been ruled by a great passion – to become one of the lords of the clan. That had been his life-spring. And he had all but achieved it. Then everything had been broken. He had been cast out of his clan like a fish onto a dry, sandy beach, panting. Clearly his personal god or *chi* was not made for great things. A man could not rise beyond the destiny of his *chi*. The saying of the elders was not true – that if a man said yea his *chi* also affirmed. Here was a man whose *chi* said nay despite his own affirmation.

The old man, Uchendu, saw clearly that Okonkwo had yielded to despair and he was greatly troubled. He would speak to him after the *isa-ifi* ceremony.

The youngest of Uchendu's five sons, Amikwu, was marrying a new wife. The bride-price had been paid and all but the last ceremony had been performed. Amikwu and his people had taken palm-wine to the bride's kinsmen about two moons before Okonkwo's arrival in Mbanta. And so it was time for the final ceremony of confession.

The daughters of the family were all there, some of them having come a long way from their homes in distant villages. Uchendu's eldest daughter had come from Obodo, nearly half a day's journey away. The daughters of Uchendu's brothers were also there. It was a full gathering of *umuada*, in the same way as they would meet if a death occurred in the family. There were twenty-two of them.

They sat in a big circle on the ground and the bride sat in the center with a hen in her right hand. Uchendu sat by her, holding the ancestral staff of the family. All the other men stood outside the circle, watching. Their wives watched also. It was evening and the sun was setting.

Uchendu's eldest daughter, Njide, asked the questions.

'Remember that if you do not answer truthfully you will suffer or even die at childbirth,' she began. 'How many men have lain with you since my brother first expressed the desire to marry you?'

'None,' she answered simply.

'Answer truthfully,' urged the other women.

'None?' asked Njide.

'None,' she answered.

'Swear on this staff of my fathers,' said Uchendu.

'I swear,' said the bride.

Uchendu took the hen from her, slit its throat with a sharp knife and allowed some of the blood to fall on his ancestral staff.

From that day Amikwu took the young bride to his hut and she became his wife. The daughters of the family did not return to their homes immediately but spent two or three days with their kinsmen.

On the second day Uchendu called together his sons and daughters and his nephew, Okonkwo. The men brought their goatskin mats, with which they sat on the floor, and the women sat on a sisal mat spread on a raised bank of earth. Uchendu pulled gently at his gray beard and gnashed his teeth. Then he began to speak, quietly and deliberately, picking his words with great care:

'It is Okonkwo that I primarily wish to speak to,' he began. 'But I want all of you to note what I am going to say. I am an old man and you are all children. I know more about the world than any of you. If there is any one among you who thinks he knows more let him speak up.' He paused, but no one spoke.

'Why is Okonkwo with us today? This is not his clan. We are only his mother's kinsmen. He does not belong here. He is an exile, condemned for seven years to live in a strange land. And so he is bowed with grief. But there is just one question I would like to ask him. Can you tell me, Okonkwo, why it is that one of the commonest names we give our children is Nneka, or "Mother is Supreme"? We all know that a man is the head of the family and his wives do his bidding. A child belongs to its father and his family and not to its mother and her family. A man belongs to his fatherland and not to his motherland. And yet we say Nneka – "Mother is Supreme." Why is that?'

There was silence. 'I want Okonkwo to answer me,' said Uchendu.

'I do not know the answer,' Okonkwo replied.

'You do not know the answer? So you see that you are a child. You have many wives and many children – more children than I have. You are a great man in your clan. But you are still a child, *my* child. Listen to me and I shall tell you. But there is one more question I shall ask you. Why is it that when a woman dies she is taken home to be buried with her own kinsmen? She is not buried with her husband's kinsmen. Why is that? Your mother was brought home to me and buried with my people. Why was that?'

Okonkwo shook his head.

'He does not know that either,' said Uchendu, 'and yet he is full of sorrow because he has come to live in his motherland for a few years.' He laughed a mirthless laughter, and turned to his sons and daughters. 'What about you? Can you answer my question?'

They all shook their heads.

'Then listen to me,' he said and cleared his throat. 'It's true that a child belongs to its father. But when a father beats his child, it seeks sympathy in its mother's hut. A man belongs to his fatherland when things are good and life is sweet. But when there is sorrow and bitterness he finds refuge in his motherland. Your mother is there to protect you. She is buried there. And that is why we say that mother is supreme. Is it right that you, Okonkwo, should bring to your mother a heavy face and refuse to be comforted? Be careful or you may displease the dead. Your duty is to comfort your wives and children and take them back to your fatherland after seven years. But if you allow sorrow to weigh you down and kill you, they will all die in exile.' He paused for a long while. 'These are now your kinsmen.' He waved at his sons and daughters. 'You think you are the greatest sufferer in the world? Do you know that men are sometimes banished for life? Do you know that men sometimes lose all their yams and even their children? I had six wives once. I have none now except that young girl who knows not her right from her left. Do you know how many children I have buried – children I begot in my youth and strength? Twenty-two. I did not hang myself, and I am still alive. If you think you are the greatest sufferer in the world ask my daughter, Akueni, how many twins she has borne and thrown away. Have you not heard the song they sing when a woman dies?

 ' "For whom is it well, for whom is it well?
 There is no one for whom it is well."

'I have no more to say to you.'

Fifteen

IT was in the second year of Okonkwo's exile that his friend, Obierika, came to visit him. He brought with him two young men, each of them carrying a heavy bag on his head. Okonkwo helped them put down their loads. It was clear that the bags were full of cowries.

Okonkwo was very happy to receive his friend. His wives and children were very happy too, and so were his cousins and their wives when he sent for them and told them who his guest was.

'You must take him to salute our father,' said one of the cousins.

'Yes,' replied Okonkwo. 'We are going directly.' But before they went he whispered something to his first wife. She nodded, and soon the children were chasing one of their cocks.

Uchendu had been told by one of his grand-children that three strangers had come to Okonkwo's house. He was therefore waiting to receive them. He held out his hands to them when they came into his *obi*, and after they had shaken hands he asked Okonkwo who they were.

'This is Obierika, my great friend. I have already spoken to you about him.'

'Yes,' said the old man, turning to Obierika. 'My son has told me about you, and I am happy you have come to see us. I knew your father, Iweka. He was a great man. He had many friends here and came to see them quite often. Those were good days when a man had friends in distant clans. Your generation does not know that. You stay at home, afraid of your next-door neighbor. Even a man's motherland is strange to him nowadays.' He looked at Okonkwo. 'I am an old man and I like to talk. That is all I am good for now.' He got up painfully, went into an inner room and came back with a kola nut.

'Who are the young men with you?' he asked as he sat down again on his goatskin. Okonkwo told him.

'Ah,' he said. 'Welcome, my sons.' He presented the kola nut to them, and when they had seen it and thanked him, he broke it and they ate.

'Go into that room,' he said to Okonkwo, pointing with his finger. 'You will find a pot of wine there.'

Okonkwo brought the wine and they began to drink. It was a day old, and very strong.

'Yes,' said Uchendu after a long silence. 'People traveled more in those days. There is not a single clan in these parts that I do not know very well. Aninta, Umuazu, Ikeocha, Elumelu, Abame – I know them all.'

'Have you heard,' asked Obierika, 'that Abame is no more?'

'How is that?' asked Uchendu and Okonkwo together.

'Abame has been wiped out,' said Obierika. 'It is a strange and terrible story. If I had not seen the few survivors with my own eyes and heard their story with my own ears, I would not have believed. Was it not on an Eke day that they fled into Umuofia?' he asked his two companions, and they nodded their heads.

'Three moons ago,' said Obierika, 'on an Eke market day a little band of fugitives came into our town. Most of them were sons of our land whose mothers had been buried with us. But there were some too who came because they had friends in our town, and others who could think of nowhere else open to escape. And so they fled into Umuofia with a woeful story.' He drank his palm-wine, and Okonkwo filled his horn again. He continued:

'During the last planting season a white man had appeared in their clan.'

'An albino,' suggested Okonkwo.

'He was not an albino. He was quite different.' He sipped his wine. 'And he was riding an iron horse. The first people who saw him ran away, but he stood beckoning to them. In the end the fearless ones went near and even touched him. The elders consulted their Oracle and it told them that the strange man would break their clan and spread destruction among them.' Obierika again drank a little of his wine. 'And so they killed the white man and tied his iron horse to their sacred tree because it looked as if it would run away to call the man's friends. I forgot to tell you another thing which the Oracle said. It said that other white men were on their way. They were locusts, it said, and that first man was their harbinger sent to explore the terrain. And so they killed him.'

'What did the white man say before they killed him?' asked Uchendu.

'He said nothing,' answered one of Obierika's companions.

'He said something, only they did not understand him,' said Obierika. 'He seemed to speak through his nose.'

'One of the men told me,' said Obierika's other companion, 'that he repeated over and over again a word that resembled Mbaino. Perhaps he had been going to Mbaino and had lost his way.'

'Anyway,' resumed Obierika, 'they killed him and tied up his iron horse. This was before the planting season began. For a long time nothing happened. The rains had come and yams had been sown. The iron horse was still tied to the sacred silk-cotton tree. And then one morning three white men led by a band of ordinary men like us came to the clan. They saw the iron horse and went away again. Most of the men and women of Abame had gone to their farms. Only a few of them saw these white men and their followers. For many market weeks nothing else happened. They have a big market in Abame on every other Afo day and, as you know, the whole clan gathers there. That was the day it happened. The three white men and a very large number of other men surrounded the market. They must have used a powerful medicine to make themselves invisible until the market was full. And they began to shoot. Everybody was killed, except the old and the sick who were at home and a handful of men and women whose *chi* were wide awake and brought them out of that market.' He paused.

'Their clan is now completely empty. Even the sacred fish in their mysterious lake have fled and the lake has turned the color of blood. A great evil has come upon their land as the Oracle had warned.'

There was a long silence. Uchendu ground his teeth together audibly. Then he burst out:

'Never kill a man who says nothing. Those men of Abame were fools. What did they know about the man?' He ground his teeth again and told a story to illustrate his point. 'Mother Kite once sent her daughter to bring food. She went, and brought back a duckling. "You have done very well," said Mother Kite to her daughter, "but tell me, what did the mother of this duckling say when you swooped and carried its child away?" "It said nothing," replied the young kite. "It just walked away." "You must return the duckling," said Mother Kite. "There is something ominous behind the silence." And so Daughter

121

Kite returned the duckling and took a chick instead. "What did the mother of this chick do?" asked the old kite. "It cried and raved and cursed me," said the young kite. "Then we can eat the chick," said her mother. "There is nothing to fear from someone who shouts." Those men of Abame were fools.'

'They were fools,' said Okonkwo after a pause. 'They had been warned that danger was ahead. They should have armed themselves with their guns and their machetes even when they went to market.'

'They have paid for their foolishness,' said Obierika. 'But I am greatly afraid. We have heard stories about white men who made the powerful guns and the strong drinks and took slaves away across the seas, but no one thought the stories were true.'

'There is no story that is not true,' said Uchendu. 'The world has no end, and what is good among one people is an abomination with others. We have albinos among us. Do you not think that they came to our clan by mistake, that they have strayed from their way to a land where everybody is like them?'

Okonkwo's first wife soon finished her cooking and set before their guests a big meal of pounded yams and bitter-leaf soup. Okonkwo's son, Nwoye, brought in a pot of sweet wine tapped from the raffia palm.

'You are a big man now,' Obierika said to Nwoye. 'Your friend Anene asked me to greet you.'

'Is he well?' asked Nwoye.

'We are all well,' said Obierika.

Ezinma brought them a bowl of water with which to wash their hands. After that they began to eat and to drink the wine.

'When did you set out from home?' asked Okonkwo.

'We had meant to set out from my house before cock-crow,' said Obierika. 'But Nweke did not appear until it was quite light. Never make an early morning appointment with a man who has just married a new wife.' They all laughed.

'Has Nweke married a wife?' asked Okonkwo.

'He has married Okadigbo's second daughter,' said Obierika.

'That is very good,' said Okonkwo. 'I do not blame you for not hearing the cock crow.'

When they had eaten, Obierika pointed at the two heavy bags.

'That is the money from your yams,' he said. 'I sold the big ones as soon as you left. Later on I sold some of the seed-yams and gave out others to share-croppers. I shall do that every year until you return. But I thought you would need the money now and so I brought it. Who knows what may happen tomorrow? Perhaps green men will come to our clan and shoot us.'

'God will not permit it,' said Okonkwo. 'I do not know how to thank you.'

'I can tell you,' said Obierika. 'Kill one of your sons for me.'

'That will not be enough,' said Okonkwo.

'Then kill yourself,' said Obierika.

'Forgive me,' said Okonkwo, smiling. 'I shall not talk about thanking you any more.'

Sixteen

WHEN nearly two years later Obierika paid another visit to his friend in exile the circumstances were less happy. The missionaries had come to Umuofia. They had built their church there, won a handful of converts and were already sending evangelists to the surrounding towns and villages. That was a source of great sorrow to the leaders of the clan; but many of them believed that the strange faith and the white man's god would not last. None of his converts was a man whose word was heeded in the assembly of the people. None of them was a man of title. They were mostly the kind of people that were called *efulefu*, worthless, empty men. The imagery of an *efulefu* in the language of the clan was a man who sold his machete and wore the sheath to battle. Chielo, the priestess of Agbala, called the converts the excrement of the clan, and the new faith was a mad dog that had come to eat it up.

What moved Obierika to visit Okonkwo was the sudden appearance of the latter's son, Nwoye, among the missionaries in Umuofia.

'What are you doing here?' Obierika had asked when after many difficulties the missionaries had allowed him to speak to the boy.

'I am one of them,' replied Nwoye.

'How is your father?' Obierika asked, not knowing what else to say.

'I don't know. He is not my father,' said Nwoye, unhappily.

And so Obierika went to Mbanta to see his friend. And he found that Okonkwo did not wish to speak about Nwoye. It was only from Nwoye's mother that he heard scraps of the story.

The arrival of the missionaries had caused a considerable stir in the village of Mbanta. There were six of them and one was a white man. Every man and woman came out to see the white man. Stories about these strange men had grown since one of them had been killed in Abame and his iron horse tied to the sacred silk-cotton tree. And so everybody came to see the white man. It was the time of the year when everybody was at home. The harvest was over.

When they had all gathered, the white man began to speak to them. He spoke through an interpreter who was an Ibo man, though his dialect was different and harsh to the ears of Mbanta. Many people laughed at his dialect and the way he used words strangely. Instead of saying 'myself' he always said 'my buttocks.' But he was a man of commanding presence and the clansmen listened to him. He said he was one of them, as they could see from his color and his language. The other four black men were also their brothers, although one of them did not speak Ibo. The white man was also their brother because they were all sons of God. And he told them about this new God, the Creator of all the world and all the men and women. He told them that they worshipped false gods, gods of wood and stone. A deep murmur went through the crowd when he said this. He told them that the true God lived on high and that all men when they died went before Him for judgment. Evil men and all the heathen who in their blindness bowed to wood and stone were thrown into a fire that burned like palm-oil. But good men who worshipped the true God lived forever in His happy kingdom. 'We have been sent by this great God to ask you to leave your wicked ways and false gods and turn to Him so that you may be saved when you die,' he said.

'Your buttocks understand our language,' said someone light-heartedly and the crowd laughed.

'What did he say?' the white man asked his interpreter. But before he could answer, another man asked a question: 'Where is the white man's horse?' he asked. The Ibo evangelists consulted among themselves and decided that the man probably meant bicycle. They told the white man and he smiled benevolently.

'Tell them,' he said, 'that I shall bring many iron horses when we have settled down among them. Some of them will even ride the iron horse themselves.' This was interpreted to them but very few of them heard. They were talking excitedly among themselves because the white man had said he was going to live among them. They had not thought about that.

At this point an old man said he had a question. 'Which is this god of yours,' he asked, 'the goddess of the earth, the god of the sky, Amadiora or the thunderbolt, or what?'

The interpreter spoke to the white man and he immediately gave his answer. 'All the gods you have named are not gods at all. They are gods of deceit who tell you to kill your fellows and destroy innocent children. There is only one true God and He has the earth, the sky, you and me and all of us.'

'If we leave our gods and follow your god,' asked another man, 'who will protect us from the anger of our neglected gods and ancestors?'

'Your gods are not alive and cannot do you any

harm,' replied the white man. 'They are pieces of wood and stone.'

When this was interpreted to the men of Mbanta they broke into derisive laughter. These men must be mad, they said to themselves. How else could they say that Ani and Amadiora were harmless? And Idemili and Ogwugwu too? And some of them began to go away.

Then the missionaries burst into song. It was one of those gay and rollicking tunes of evangelism which had the power of plucking at silent and dusty chords in the heart of an Ibo man. The interpreter explained each verse to the audience, some of whom now stood enthralled. It was a story of brothers who lived in darkness and in fear, ignorant of the love of God. It told of one sheep out on the hills, away from the gates of God and from the tender shepherd's care.

After the singing the interpreter spoke about the Son of God whose name was Jesu Kristi. Okonkwo, who only stayed in the hope that it might come to chasing the men out of the village or whipping them, now said:

'You told us with your own mouth that there was only one god. Now you talk about his son. He must have a wife, then.' The crowd agreed.

'I did not say He had a wife,' said the interpreter, somewhat lamely.

'Your buttocks said he had a son,' said the joker. 'So he must have a wife and all of them must have buttocks.'

The missionary ignored him and went on to talk about the Holy Trinity. At the end of it Okonkwo was fully convinced that the man was mad. He shrugged his shoulders and went away to tap his afternoon palm-wine.

But there was a young lad who had been captivated. His name was Nwoye, Okonkwo's first son. It was not the mad logic of the Trinity that captivated him. He did not understand it. It was the poetry of the new religion, something felt in the marrow. The hymn about brothers who sat in darkness and in fear seemed to answer a vague and persistent question that haunted his young soul – the question of the twins crying in the bush and the question of Ikemefuna who was killed. He felt a relief within as the hymn poured into his parched soul. The words of the hymn were like the drops of frozen rain melting on the dry palate of the panting earth. Nwoye's callow mind was greatly puzzled.

Seventeen

THE missionaries spent their first four or five nights in the market place, and went into the village in the morning to preach the gospel. They asked who the king of the village was, but the villagers told them that there was no king. 'We have men of high title and the chief priests and the elders,' they said.

It was not very easy getting the men of high title and the elders together after the excitement of the first day. But the missionaries persevered, and in the end they were received by the rulers of Mbanta. They asked for a plot of land to build their church.

Every clan and village had its 'evil forest.' In it were buried all those who died of the really evil diseases, like leprosy and smallpox. It was also the dumping ground for the potent fetishes of great medicine men when they died. An 'evil forest' was, therefore, alive with sinister forces and powers of darkness. It was such a forest that the rulers of Mbanta gave to the missionaries. They did not really want them in their clan, and so they made them that offer which nobody in his right senses would accept.

'They want a piece of land to build their shrine,' said Uchendu to his peers when they consulted among themselves. 'We shall give them a piece of land.' He paused, and there was a murmur of surprise and disagreement. 'Let us give them a portion of the Evil Forest. They boast about victory over death. Let us give them a real battlefield in which to show their victory.' They laughed and agreed, and sent for the missionaries, whom they had asked to leave them for a while so that they might 'whisper together.' They offered them as much of the Evil Forest as they cared to take. And to their greatest amazement the missionaries thanked them and burst into song.

'They do not understand,' said some of the elders. 'But they will understand when they go to their plot of land tomorrow morning.' And they dispersed.

The next morning the crazy men actually began to clear a part of the forest and to build their house. The inhabitants of Mbanta expected them all to be dead within four days. The first day passed and the second and third and fourth, and none of them died. Everyone was puzzled. And then it became known that the white man's fetish had unbelievable power. It was said that he wore glasses on his eyes so that he could see and talk to evil spirits. Not long after, he won his first three converts.

Although Nwoye had been attracted to the new faith from the very first day, he kept it secret. He dared not go too near the missionaries for fear of his father. But whenever they came to preach in the open market place or the village playground, Nwoye was there. And he was already beginning to know some of the simple stories they told.

'We have now built a church,' said Mr. Kiaga, the interpreter, who was now in charge of the infant congregation. The white man had gone back to Umuofia, where he built his headquarters and from where he paid regular visits to Mr. Kiaga's congregation at Mbanta.

'We have now built a church,' said Mr. Kiaga, 'and we want you all to come in every seventh day to worship the true God.'

On the following Sunday, Nwoye passed and re-passed the little red-earth and thatch building without summoning enough courage to enter. He heard the voice of singing and although it came from a handful of men it was loud and confident. Their church stood on a circular clearing that looked like the open mouth of the Evil Forest. Was it waiting to snap its teeth together? After passing and re-passing by the church, Nwoye returned home.

It was well known among the people of Mbanta that their gods and ancestors were sometimes long-suffering and would deliberately allow a man to go on defying them. But even in such cases they set their limit at seven market weeks or twenty-eight days. Beyond that limit no man was suffered to go. And so excitement mounted in the village as the seventh week approached since the impudent missionaries built their church in the Evil Forest. The villagers were so certain about the doom that awaited these men that one or two converts thought it wise to suspend their allegiance to the new faith.

At last the day came by which all the missionaries should have died. But they were still alive, building a new red-earth and thatch house for their teacher, Mr. Kiaga. That week they won a handful more converts. And for the first time they had a woman. Her name was Nneka, the wife of Amadi, who was a prosperous farmer. She was very heavy with child.

Nneka had had four previous pregnancies and childbirths. But each time she had borne twins, and they had been immediately thrown away. Her husband and his family were already becoming highly critical of such a woman and were not unduly perturbed when they found she had fled to join the Christians. It was a good riddance.

One morning Okonkwo's cousin, Amikwu, was passing by the church on his way from the neighboring village, when he saw Nwoye among the Christians. He was greatly surprised, and when he got home he went straight to Okonkwo's hut and told him what he had seen. The women began to talk excitedly, but Okonkwo sat unmoved.

It was late afternoon before Nwoye returned. He went into the *obi* and saluted his father, but he did not answer. Nwoye turned round to walk into the inner compound when his father, suddenly overcome with fury, sprang to his feet and gripped him by the neck.

'Where have you been?' he stammered.

Nwoye struggled to free himself from the choking grip.

'Answer me,' roared Okonkwo, 'before I kill you!' He seized a heavy stick that lay on the dwarf wall and hit him two or three savage blows.

'Answer me!' he roared again. Nwoye stood looking at him and did not say a word. The women were screaming outside, afraid to go in.

'Leave that boy at once!' said a voice in the outer compound. It was Okonkwo's uncle, Uchendu. 'Are you mad?'

Okonkwo did not answer. But he left hold of Nwoye, who walked away and never returned.

He went back to the church and told Mr. Kiaga that he had decided to go to Umuofia where the white missionary had set up a school to teach young Christians to read and write.

Mr. Kiaga's joy was very great. 'Blessed is he who forsakes his father and his mother for my sake,' he intoned. 'Those that hear my words are my father and my mother.'

Nwoye did not fully understand. But he was happy to leave his father. He would return later to his mother and his brothers and sisters and convert them to the new faith.

As Okonkwo sat in his hut that night, gazing into a log fire, he thought over the matter. A sudden fury rose within him and he felt a strong desire to take up his machete, go to the church and wipe out the entire vile and miscreant gang. But on further thought he told himself that Nwoye was not worth fighting for. Why, he cried in his heart, should he, Okonkwo, of all people, be cursed with such a son? He saw clearly in it the finger of his personal god or *chi*. For how else could he explain his great misfortune and exile and now his despicable son's behavior? Now that he had time to think of it, his son's crime stood out in its stark enormity. To abandon the gods of one's father and go about with a lot of effeminate men clucking like old hens was the very depth of abomination. Suppose when he died all his male children decided to follow Nwoye's steps and abandon their ancestors? Okonkwo felt a cold shudder run through him at the terrible prospects, like the prospect of annihilation. He saw himself and his fathers crowding round their ancestral shrine waiting in vain for worship and sacrifice and finding nothing but ashes of bygone days, and his children the while praying to the white man's god. If such a thing were ever to happen, he, Okonkwo, would wipe them off the face of the earth.

Okonkwo was popularly called the 'Roaring Flame.' As he looked into the log fire he recalled the name. He was a flaming fire. How then could he have begotten a son like Nwoye, degenerate and effeminate? Perhaps he was not his son. No! he could not be. His wife had played him false. He would teach her! But Nwoye resembled his grandfather, Unoka, who was Okonkwo's father. He pushed the thought out of his mind. He, Okonkwo, was called a flaming fire. How could he have begotten a woman for a son? At Nwoye's age Okonkwo had already become famous throughout Umuofia for his wrestling and his fearlessness.

He sighed heavily, and as if in sympathy the smoldering log also sighed. And immediately Okonkwo's eyes were opened and he saw the whole matter clearly. Living fire begets cold, impotent ash. He sighed again, deeply.

Eighteen

THE young church in Mbanta had a few crises early in its life. At first the clan had assumed that it would not survive. But it had gone on living and gradually becoming stronger. The clan was worried, but not overmuch. If a gang of *efulefu* decided to live in the Evil Forest it was their own affair. When one came to think of it, the Evil Forest was a fit home for such undesirable people. It was true they were rescuing twins from the bush, but they never brought them into the village. As far as the villagers were concerned, the twins still remained where they had been thrown away. Surely the earth goddess would not visit the sins of the missionaries on the innocent villagers?

But on one occasion the missionaries had tried to overstep the bounds. Three converts had gone into the village and boasted openly that all the gods were dead and impotent and that they were prepared to defy them by burning all their shrines.

'Go and burn your mothers' genitals,' said one of the priests. The men were seized and beaten until they streamed with blood. After that nothing happened for a long time between the church and the clan.

But stories were already gaining ground that the white man had not only brought a religion but also a government. It was said that they had built a place of judgment in Umuofia to protect the followers of their religion. It was even said that they had hanged one man who killed a missionary.

Although such stories were now often told they looked like fairy-tales in Mbanta and did not as yet affect the relationship between the new church and the clan. There was no question of killing a missionary here, for Mr. Kiaga, despite his madness, was quite harmless. As for his converts, no one could kill them without having to flee from the clan, for in spite of their worthlessness they still belonged to the clan. And so nobody gave serious thought to the stories about the white man's government or the consequences of killing the Christians. If they became more troublesome than they already were they would simply be driven out of the clan.

And the little church was at that moment too deeply absorbed in its own troubles to annoy the clan. It all began over the question of admitting outcasts.

These outcasts, or *osu*, seeing that the new religion welcomed twins and such abominations, thought that it was possible that they would also be received. And so one Sunday two of them went into the church. There was an immediate stir; but so great was the work the new religion had done among the converts that they did not immediately leave the church when the outcasts came in. Those who found themselves nearest to them merely moved to another seat. It was a miracle. But it only lasted till the end of the service. The whole church raised a protest and was about to drive these people out, when Mr. Kiaga stopped them and began to explain.

'Before God,' he said, 'there is no slave or free. We are all children of God and we must receive these our brothers.'

'You do not understand,' said one of the converts. 'What will the heathen say of us when they hear that we receive *osu* into our midst? They will laugh.'

'Let them laugh,' said Mr. Kiaga. 'God will laugh at them on the judgment day. Why do the nations rage and the peoples imagine a vain thing? He that sitteth in the heavens shall laugh. The Lord shall have them in derision.'

'You do not understand,' the convert maintained. 'You are our teacher, and you can teach us the things of the new faith. But this is a matter which we know.' And he told him what an *osu* was.

He was a person dedicated to a god, a thing set apart – a taboo for ever, and his children after him. He could neither marry nor be married by the free-born. He was in fact an outcast, living in a special area of the village, close to the Great Shrine. Wherever he went he carried with him the mark of his forbidden caste – long, tangled and dirty hair. A razor was taboo to him. An *osu* could not attend an assembly of the free-born, and they, in turn, could not shelter under his roof. He could not take any of the four titles of the clan, and when he died he was buried by his kind in the Evil Forest. How could such a man be a follower of Christ?

'He needs Christ more than you and I,' said Mr. Kiaga.

'Then I shall go back to the clan,' said the convert. And he went. Mr. Kiaga stood firm, and it was his firmness that saved the young church. The wavering converts drew inspiration and confidence from his unshakable faith. He ordered the outcasts to shave off their long, tangled hair. At first they were afraid they might die.

'Unless you shave off the mark of your heathen belief I will not admit you into the church,' said Mr. Kiaga. 'You fear that you will die. Why should that be? How are you different from other men who shave their hair? The same God created you and them. But they have cast you out like lepers. It is against the will of God, who has promised everlasting life to all who believe in His holy name. The heathen say you will die if you do this or that, and you are afraid. They also said I would die if I built my church on this ground. Am I dead? They said I would die if I took care of twins. I am still alive. The heathen speak nothing but falsehood. Only the word of our God is true.'

The two outcasts shaved off their hair, and soon they were the strongest adherents of the new faith. And what was more, nearly all the *osu* in Mbanta followed their example. It was in fact one of them who in his zeal brought the church into serious conflict with the clan a year later by killing the sacred python, the emanation of the god of water.

The royal python was the most revered animal in Mbanta and all the surrounding clans. It was addressed as 'Our Father,' and was allowed to go wherever it chose, even into people's beds. It ate rats in the house and sometimes swallowed hens' eggs. If a clansman killed a royal python accidentally, he made sacrifices of atonement and performed an expensive burial ceremony such as was done for a great man. No punishment was prescribed for a man who killed the python knowingly. Nobody thought that such a thing could ever happen.

Perhaps it never did happen. That was the way the clan at first looked at it. No one had actually seen the man do it. The story had arisen among the Christians themselves.

But, all the same, the rulers and elders of Mbanta assembled to decide on their action. Many of them spoke at great length and in fury. The spirit of war was upon them. Okonkwo, who had begun to play a part in the affairs of his motherland, said that until the abominable gang was chased out of the village with whips there would be no peace.

But there were many others who saw the situation differently, and it was their counsel that prevailed in the end.

'It is not our custom to fight for our gods,' said one of them. 'Let us not presume to do so now. If a man kills the sacred python in the secrecy of his hut, the matter lies between him and the god. We did not see it. If we put ourselves between the god and his victim we may receive blows intended for the offender. When a man blasphemes, what do we do? Do we go and stop his mouth? No. We put our fingers into our ears to stop us hearing. That is a wise action.'

'Let us not reason like cowards,' said Okonkwo. 'If a man comes into my hut and defecates on the floor, what do I do? Do I shut my eyes? No! I take a stick and break his head. That is what a man does. These people are daily pouring filth over us, and Okeke says we should pretend not to see.' Okonkwo made a sound full of disgust. This was a womanly clan, he thought. Such a thing could never happen in his fatherland, Umuofia.

'Okonkwo has spoken the truth,' said another man. 'We should do something. But let us ostracize these men. We would then not be held accountable for their abominations.'

Everybody in the assembly spoke, and in the end it was decided to ostracize the Christians. Okonkwo ground his teeth in disgust.

That night a bell-man went through the length and breadth of Mbanta proclaiming that the adherents of the new faith were thenceforth excluded from the life and privileges of the clan.

The Christians had grown in number and were now a small community of men, women and children, self-assured and confident. Mr. Brown, the white missionary, paid regular visits to them. 'When I think that it is only eighteen months since the Seed was first sown among you,' he said, 'I marvel at what the Lord hath wrought.'

It was Wednesday in Holy Week and Mr. Kiaga had asked the women to bring red earth and white chalk and water to scrub the church for Easter; and the women had formed themselves into three groups for this purpose. They set out early that morning, some of them with their water-pots to the stream, another group with hoes and baskets to the village red-earth pit, and the others to the chalk quarry.

Mr. Kiaga was praying in the church when he heard the women talking excitedly. He rounded off his prayer and went to see what it was all about. The women had come to the church with empty water-pots. They said that some young men had chased them away from the stream with whips. Soon after, the women who had gone for red earth returned with empty baskets. Some of them had been heavily whipped. The chalk women also returned to tell a similar story.

'What does it all mean?' asked Mr. Kiaga, who was greatly perplexed.

'The village has outlawed us,' said one of the women. 'The bell-man announced it last night. But it is not our custom to debar anyone from the stream or the quarry.'

Another woman said, 'They want to ruin us. They will not allow us into the markets. They have said so.'

Mr. Kiaga was going to send into the village for his men-converts when he saw them coming on their own. Of course they had all heard the bell-man, but they had never in all their lives heard of women being debarred from the stream.

'Come along,' they said to the women. 'We will go with you to meet those cowards.' Some of them had big sticks and some even machetes.

But Mr. Kiaga restrained them. He wanted first to know why they had been outlawed.

'They say that Okoli killed the sacred python,' said one man.

'It is false,' said another. 'Okoli told me himself that it was false.'

Okoli was not there to answer. He had fallen ill on the previous night. Before the day was over he was dead. His death showed that the gods were still able to fight their own battles. The clan saw no reason then for molesting the Christians.

Nineteen

THE last big rains of the year were falling. It was the time for treading red earth with which to build walls. It was not done earlier because the rains were too heavy and would have washed away the heap of trodden earth; and it could not be done later because harvesting would soon set in, and after that the dry season.

It was going to be Okonkwo's last harvest in Mbanta. The seven wasted and weary years were at last dragging to a close. Although he had prospered in his motherland Okonkwo knew that he would have prospered even more in Umuofia, in the land of his fathers where men were bold and warlike. In these seven years he would have climbed to the utmost heights. And so he regretted every day of his exile. His mother's kinsmen had been very kind to him, and he was grateful. But that did not alter the facts. He had called the first child born to him in exile Nneka – 'Mother is Supreme' – out of politeness to his mother's kinsmen. But two years later when a son was born he called him Nwofia – 'Begotten in the Wilderness.'

As soon as he entered his last year in exile Okonkwo sent money to Obierika to build him two huts in his old compound where he and his family would live until he built more huts and the outside wall of his compound. He could not ask another man to build his own *obi* for him, nor the walls of his compound. Those things a man built for himself or inherited from his father.

As the last heavy rains of the year began to fall, Obierika sent word that the two huts had been built and Okonkwo began to prepare for his return, after the rains. He would have liked to return earlier and build his compound that year before the rains stopped, but in doing so he would have taken something from the full penalty of seven years. And that could not be. So he waited impatiently for the dry season to come.

It came slowly. The rain became lighter and lighter until it fell in slanting showers. Sometimes the sun shone through the rain and a light breeze blew. It was a gay and airy kind of rain. The rainbow began to appear, and sometimes two rainbows, like a mother and her daughter, the one young and beautiful, and the other an old and faint shadow. The rainbow was called the python of the sky.

Okonkwo called his three wives and told them to get things together for a great feast. 'I must thank my mother's kinsmen before I go,' he said.

Ekwefi still had some cassava left on her farm from the previous year. Neither of the other wives had. It was not that they had been lazy, but that they had many children to feed. It was therefore understood that Ekwefi would provide cassava for the feast. Nwoye's mother and Ojiugo would provide the other things like smoked fish, palm-oil and pepper for the soup. Okonkwo would take care of meat and yams.

Ekwefi rose early on the following morning and went to her farm with her daughter, Ezinma, and Ojiugo's daughter, Obiageli, to harvest cassava tubers. Each of them carried a long cane basket, a machete for cutting down the soft cassava stem, and a little hoe for digging out the tuber. Fortunately, a light rain had fallen during the night and the soil would not be very hard.

'It will not take us long to harvest as much as we like,' said Ekwefi.

'But the leaves will be wet,' said Ezinma. Her basket was balanced on her head, and her arms folded across her breasts. She felt cold. 'I dislike cold water dropping on my back. We should have waited for the sun to rise and dry the leaves.'

Obiageli called her 'Salt' because she said that she disliked water. 'Are you afraid you may dissolve?'

The harvesting was easy, as Ekwefi had said. Ezinma shook every tree violently with a long stick before she bent down to cut the stem and dig out the tuber. Sometimes it was not necessary to dig. They just pulled the stump, and earth rose, roots snapped below, and the tuber was pulled out.

When they had harvested a sizable heap they carried it down in two trips to the stream, where every woman had a shallow well for fermenting her cassava.

'It should be ready in four days or even three,' said Obiageli. 'They are young tubers.'

'They are not all that young,' said Ekwefi. 'I planted the farm nearly two years ago. It is a poor soil and that is why the tubers are so small.'

Okonkwo never did things by halves. When his wife Ekwefi protested that two goats were sufficient for the feast he told her that it was not her affair.

'I am calling a feast because I have the wherewithal. I cannot live on the bank of a river and wash my hands with spittle. My mother's people have been good to me and I must show my gratitude.'

And so three goats were slaughtered and a number of fowls. It was like a wedding feast. There was foo-foo and yam pottage, egusi soup and bitter-leaf soup and pots and pots of palm-wine.

All the *umunna* were invited to the feast, all the descendants of Okolo, who had lived about two hundred years before. The oldest member of this extensive family was Okonkwo's uncle, Uchendu. The kola nut was given to him to break, and he prayed to the ancestors. He asked them for health and children. 'We do not ask for wealth because he that has health and children will also have wealth. We do not pray to have more money but to have more kinsmen. We are better than animals because we have kinsmen. An animal rubs its itching flank against a tree, a man asks his kinsman to scratch him.' He prayed especially for Okonkwo and his family. He then broke the kola nut and threw one of the lobes on the ground for the ancestors.

As the broken kola nuts were passed round, Okonkwo's wives and children and those who came to help them with the cooking began to bring out the food. His sons brought out the pots of palm-wine. There was so much food and drink that many kinsmen whistled in surprise. When all was laid out, Okonkwo rose to speak.

'I beg you to accept this little kola,' he said. 'It is not to pay you back for all you did for me in these seven years. A child cannot pay for its mother's milk. I have only called you together because it is good for kinsmen to meet.'

Yam pottage was served first because it was lighter than foo-foo and because yam always came first. Then the foo-foo was served. Some kinsmen ate it with egusi soup and others with bitter-leaf soup. The meat was then shared so that every member of the *umunna* had a portion. Every man rose in order of years and took a share. Even the few kinsmen who had not been able to come had their shares taken out for them in due term.

As the palm-wine was drunk one of the oldest members of the *umunna* rose to thank Okonkwo:

'If I say that we did not expect such a big feast I will be suggesting that we did not know how open-handed our son, Okonkwo, is. We all know him, and we expected a big feast. But it turned out to be even bigger than we expected. Thank you. May all you took out return again tenfold. It is good in these days when the younger generation consider themselves wiser than their sires to see a man doing things in the grand, old way. A man who calls his kinsmen to a feast does not do so to save them from starving. They all have food in their own homes. When we gather together in the moonlit village ground it is not because of the moon. Every man can see it in his own compound. We come together because it is good for kinsmen to do so. You may ask why I am saying all this. I say it because I fear for the younger generation, for you people.' He waved his arm where most of the young men sat. 'As for me, I have only a short while to live, and so have Uchendu and Unachukwu and Emefo. But I fear for you young people because you do not understand how strong is the bond of kinship. You do not know what it is to speak with one voice. And what is the result? An abominable religion has settled among you. A man can now leave his father and his brothers. He can curse the gods of his fathers and his ancestors, like a hunter's dog that suddenly goes mad and turns on his master. I fear for you; I fear for the clan.' He turned again to Okonkwo and said, 'Thank you for calling us together.'

PART THREE

Twenty

SEVEN years was a long time to be away from one's clan. A man's place was not always there, waiting for him. As soon as he left, someone else rose and filled it. The clan was like a lizard; if it lost its tail it soon grew another.

Okonkwo knew these things. He knew that he had lost his place among the nine masked spirits who administered justice in the clan. He had lost the chance to lead his warlike clan against the new religion, which, he was told, had gained ground. He had lost the years in which he might have taken the highest titles in the clan. But some of these losses were not irreparable. He was determined that his return should be marked by his people. He would return with a flourish, and regain the seven wasted years.

Even in his first year in exile he had begun to plan for his return. The first thing he would do would be to rebuild his compound on a more magnificent scale. He would build a bigger barn than he had had before and he would build huts for two new wives. Then he would show his wealth by initiating his sons into the *ozo* society. Only the really great men in the clan were able to do this. Okonkwo saw clearly the high esteem in which he would be held, and he saw himself taking the highest title in the land.

As the years of exile passed one by one it seemed to him that his *chi* might now be making amends for the past disaster. His yams grew abundantly, not only in his motherland but also in Umuofia, where his friend gave them out year by year to share-croppers.

Then the tragedy of his first son had occurred. At first it appeared as if it might prove too great for his spirit. But it was a resilient spirit, and in the end Okonkwo overcame his sorrow. He had five other sons and he would bring them up in the way of the clan.

He sent for the five sons and they came and sat in his *obi*. The youngest of them was four years old.

'You have all seen the great abomination of your brother. Now he is no longer my son or your brother. I will only have a son who is a man, who will hold his head up among my people. If any one of you prefers to be a woman, let him follow Nwoye now while I am alive so that I can curse him. If you turn against me when I am dead I will visit you and break your neck.'

Okonkwo was very lucky in his daughters. He never stopped regretting that Ezinma was a girl. Of all his children she alone understood his every mood. A bond of sympathy had grown between them as the years had passed.

Ezinma grew up in her father's exile and became one of the most beautiful girls in Mbanta. She was called Crystal of Beauty, as her mother had been called in her youth. The young ailing girl who had caused her mother so much heartache had been transformed, almost overnight, into a healthy, buoyant maiden. She had, it was true, her moments of depression when she would snap at everybody like an angry dog. These moods descended on her suddenly and for no apparent reason. But they were very rare and short-lived. As long as they lasted, she could bear no other person but her father.

Many young men and prosperous middle-aged men of Mbanta came to marry her. But she refused them all, because her father had called her one evening and said to her: 'There are many good and prosperous people here, but I shall be happy if you marry in Umuofia when we return home.'

That was all he had said. But Ezinma had seen clearly all the thought and hidden meaning behind the few words. And she had agreed.

'Your half-sister, Obiageli, will not understand me,' Okonkwo said. 'But you can explain to her.'

Although they were almost the same age, Ezinma wielded a strong influence over her half-sister. She explained to her why they should not marry yet, and she agreed also. And so the two of them refused every offer of marriage in Mbanta.

'I wish she were a boy,' Okonkwo thought within himself. She understood things so perfectly. Who else among his children could have read his thoughts so well? With two beautiful grown-up daughters his return to Umuofia would attract considerable attention. His future sons-in-law would be men of authority in the clan. The poor and unknown would not dare to come forth.

Umuofia had indeed changed during the seven years Okonkwo had been in exile. The church had come and led many astray. Not only the low-born and the outcast but sometimes a worthy man had joined it. Such a man was Ogbuefi Ugonna, who had taken two titles, and who like a madman had cut the anklet of his titles and cast it away to join the Christians. The white missionary was very proud of him and he was one of the first men in Umuofia to receive the sacrament of Holy Communion, or Holy Feast as it was called in Ibo. Ogbuefi Ugonna had thought of the Feast in terms of eating and drinking, only more holy than the village variety. He had therefore put his drinking horn into his goatskin bag for the occasion.

But apart from the church, the white men had also brought a government. They had built a court where the District Commissioner judged cases in ignorance. He had court messengers who brought men to him for trial. Many of these messengers came from Umuru on the bank of the Great River, where the white men first came many years before and where they had built the center of their religion and trade and government. These court messengers were greatly hated in Umuofia because they were foreigners and also arrogant and high-handed. They were called *kotma*, and because of their ash-colored shorts they earned the additional name of Ashy-Buttocks. They guarded the prison, which was full of men who had offended against the white man's law. Some of these prisoners had thrown away their twins and some had molested the Christians. They were beaten in the prison by the *kotma* and made to work every morning clearing the government compound and fetching wood for the white Commissioner and the court messengers. Some of these prisoners were men of title who should be above such mean occupation. They were grieved by the indignity and mourned for their neglected farms. As they cut grass in the morning the younger men sang in time with the strokes of their machetes:

> '*Kotma* of the ash buttocks,
>   He is fit to be a slave.
> The white man has no sense,
>   He is fit to be a slave.'

The court messengers did not like to be called Ashy-Buttocks, and they beat the men. But the song spread in Umuofia.

Okonkwo's head was bowed in sadness as Obierika told him these things.

'Perhaps I have been away too long,' Okonkwo said, almost to himself. 'But I cannot understand these things you tell me. What is it that has happened to our people? Why have they lost the power to fight?'

'Have you not heard how the white man wiped out Abame?' asked Obierika.

'I have heard,' said Okonkwo. 'But I have also heard that Abame people were weak and foolish. Why did they not fight back? Had they no guns and machetes? We would be cowards to compare ourselves with the men of Abame. Their fathers had never dared to stand before our ancestors. We must fight these men and drive them from the land.'

'It is already too late,' said Obierika sadly. 'Our own men and our sons have joined the ranks of the stranger. They have joined his religion and they help to uphold his government. If we should try to drive out the white men in Umuofia we should find it easy. There are only two of them. But what of our own people who are following their way and have been given power? They would go to Umuru and bring the soldiers, and we would be like Abame.' He paused for a long time and then said: 'I told you on my last visit to Mbanta how they hanged Aneto.'

'What has happened to that piece of land in dispute?' asked Okonkwo.

'The white man's court has decided that it should belong to Nnama's family, who had given much money to the white man's messengers and interpreter.'

'Does the white man understand our custom about land?'

'How can he when he does not even speak our tongue? But he says that our customs are bad; and our own brothers who have taken up his religion also say that our customs are bad. How do you think we can fight when our own brothers have turned against us? The white man is very clever. He came quietly and peaceably with his religion. We were amused at his foolishness and allowed him to stay. Now he has won our brothers, and our clan can no longer act like one. He has put a knife on the things that held us together and we have fallen apart.'

'How did they get hold of Aneto to hang him?' asked Okonkwo.

'When he killed Oduche in the fight over the land, he fled to Aninta to escape the wrath of the earth. This was about eight days after the fight, because Oduche had not died immediately from his wounds. It was on the seventh day that he died. But everybody knew that he was going to die and Aneto got his belongings together in readiness to flee. But the Christians had told the white man about the accident, and he sent his *kotma* to catch Aneto. He was imprisoned with all the leaders of his family. In the end Oduche died and Aneto was taken to Umuru and hanged. The other people were released, but even now they have not found the mouth with which to tell of their suffering.'

The two men sat in silence for a long while afterwards.

Twenty-one

THERE were many men and women in Umuofia who did not feel as strongly as Okonkwo about the new dispensation. The white man had indeed brought a lunatic religion, but he had also built a trading store and for the first time palm-oil and kernel became things of great price, and much money flowed into Umuofia.

And even in the matter of religion there was a growing feeling that there might be something in it after all, something vaguely akin to method in the overwhelming madness.

This growing feeling was due to Mr. Brown, the white missionary, who was very firm in restraining his flock from provoking the wrath of the clan. One member in particular was very difficult to restrain. His name was Enoch and his father was the priest of the snake cult. The story went around that Enoch had killed and eaten the sacred python, and that his father had cursed him.

Mr. Brown preached against such excess of zeal. Everything was possible, he told his energetic flock, but everything was not expedient. And so Mr. Brown came to be respected even by the clan, because he trod softly on its faith. He made friends with some of the great men of the clan and on one of his frequent visits to the neighboring villages he had been presented with a carved elephant tusk, which was a sign of dignity and rank. One of the great men in that village was called Akunna and he had given one of his sons to be taught the white man's knowledge in Mr. Brown's school.

Whenever Mr. Brown went to that village he spent long hours with Akunna in his *obi* talking through an interpreter about religion. Neither of them succeeded in converting the other but they learned more about their different beliefs.

'You say that there is one supreme God who made heaven and earth,' said Akunna on one of Mr. Brown's visits. 'We also believe in Him and call Him Chukwu. He made all the world and the other gods.'

'There are no other gods,' said Mr. Brown. 'Chukwu is the only God and all others are false. You carve a piece of wood – like that one' (he pointed at the rafters from which Akunna's carved *Ikenga* hung), 'and you call it a god. But it is still a piece of wood.'

'Yes,' said Akunna. 'It is indeed a piece of wood. The tree from which it came was made by Chukwu, as indeed all minor gods were. But He made them for His messengers so that we could approach Him through them. It is like yourself. You are the head of your church.'

'No,' protested Mr. Brown. 'The head of my church is God Himself.'

'I know,' said Akunna, 'but there must be a head in this world among men. Somebody like yourself must be the head here.'

'The head of my church in that sense is in England.'

'That is exactly what I am saying. The head of your church is in your country. He has sent you here as his messenger. And you have also appointed your own messengers and servants. Or let me take another example, the District Commissioner. He is sent by your king.'

'They have a queen,' said the interpreter on his own account.

'Your queen sends her messenger, the District Commissioner. He finds that he cannot do the work alone and so he appoints *kotma* to help him. It is the same with God, or Chukwu. He appoints the smaller gods to help Him because His work is too great for one person.'

'You should not think of Him as a person,' said Mr. Brown. 'It is because you do so that you imagine He must need helpers. And the worst thing about it is that you give all the worship to the false gods you have created.'

'That is not so. We make sacrifices to the little gods, but when they fail and there is no one else to turn to we go to Chukwu. It is right to do so. We approach a great man through his servants. But when his servants fail to help us, then we go to the last source of hope. We appear to pay greater attention to the little gods but that is not so. We worry them more because we are afraid to worry their Master. Our fathers knew that Chukwu was the Overlord and that is why many of them gave their children the name Chukwuka – "Chukwu is Supreme."'

'You said one interesting thing,' said Mr. Brown. 'You are afraid of Chukwu. In my religion Chukwu is a loving Father and need not be feared by those who do His will.'

'But we must fear Him when we are not doing His will,' said Akunna. 'And who is to tell His will? It is too great to be known.'

In this way Mr. Brown learned a good deal about the religion of the clan and he came to the conclusion that a frontal attack on it would not succeed. And so he built a school and a little hospital in Umuofia. He went from family to family begging people to send their children to his school. But at first they only sent their slaves or sometimes their lazy children. Mr. Brown begged and argued and prophesied. He said that the leaders of the land in the future would be men and women who had learned to read and write. If Umuofia failed to send her children to the school, strangers would come from other places to rule them. They could already see that happening in the Native Court, where the D.C. was surrounded by strangers who spoke his tongue. Most of these strangers came from the distant town of Umuru on the bank of the Great River where the white man first went.

In the end Mr. Brown's arguments began to have an effect. More people came to learn in his school, and he encouraged them with gifts of singlets and towels. They were not all young, these people who came to learn. Some of them were thirty years old or more. They worked on their farms in the morning and went to school in the afternoon. And it was not long before the people began to say that the white man's medicine was quick in working. Mr. Brown's school produced quick results. A few months in it were enough to make one a court messenger or even a court clerk. Those who stayed longer became teachers; and from Umuofia laborers went forth into the Lord's vineyard. New churches were established in the surrounding villages and a few schools with them. From the very beginning religion and education went hand in hand.

Mr. Brown's mission grew from strength to strength, and because of its link with the new administration it earned a new social prestige. But Mr. Brown himself was breaking down in health. At first he ignored the warning signs. But in the end he had to leave his flock, sad and broken.

*

It was in the first rainy season after Okonkwo's return to Umuofia that Mr. Brown left for home. As soon as he had learned of Okonkwo's return five months earlier, the missionary had immediately paid him a visit. He had just sent Okonkwo's son, Nwoye, who was now called Isaac, to the new training college for teachers in Umuru. And he had hoped that Okonkwo would be happy to hear of it. But Okonkwo had driven him away with the threat that if he came into his compound again, he would be carried out of it.

Okonkwo's return to his native land was not as memorable as he had wished. It was true his two beautiful daughters aroused great interest among suitors and marriage negotiations were soon in progress, but, beyond that, Umuofia did not appear to have taken any special notice of the warrior's return. The clan had undergone such profound change during his exile that it was barely recognizable. The new religion and government and the trading stores were very much in the people's eyes and minds. There were still many who saw these new institutions as evil, but even they talked and thought about little else, and certainly not about Okonkwo's return.

And it was the wrong year too. If Okonkwo had immediately initiated his two sons into the *ozo* society as he had planned he would have caused a stir. But the initiation rite was performed once in three years in Umuofia, and he had to wait for nearly two years for the next round of ceremonies.

Okonkwo was deeply grieved. And it was not just a personal grief. He mourned for the clan, which he saw breaking up and falling apart, and he mourned for the warlike men of Umuofia, who had so unaccountably become soft like women.

Twenty-two

MR. BROWN'S successor was the Reverend James Smith, and he was a different kind of man. He condemned openly Mr. Brown's policy of compromise and accommodation. He saw things as black and white. And black was evil. He saw the world as a battlefield in which the children of light were locked in mortal conflict with the sons of darkness. He spoke in his sermons about sheep and goats and about wheat and tares. He believed in slaying the prophets of Baal.

Mr. Smith was greatly distressed by the ignorance which many of his flock showed even in such things as the Trinity and the Sacraments. It only showed that they were seeds sown on a rocky soil. Mr. Brown had thought of nothing but numbers. He should have known that the kingdom of God did not depend on large crowds. Our Lord Himself stressed the importance of fewness. Narrow is the way and few the number. To fill the Lord's holy temple with an idolatrous crowd clamoring for signs was a folly of everlasting consequence. Our Lord used the whip only once in His life – to drive the crowd away from His church.

Within a few weeks of his arrival in Umuofia Mr. Smith suspended a young woman from the church for pouring new wine into old bottles. This woman had allowed her heathen husband to mutilate her dead child. The child had been declared an *ogbanje*, plaguing its mother by dying and entering her womb to be born again. Four times this child had run its evil round. And so it was mutilated to discourage it from returning.

Mr. Smith was filled with wrath when he heard of this. He disbelieved the story which even some of the most faithful confirmed, the story of really evil children who were not deterred by mutilation, but came back with all the scars. He replied that such stories were spread in the world by the Devil to lead men astray. Those who believed such stories were unworthy of the Lord's table.

There was a saying in Umuofia that as a man danced so the drums were beaten for him. Mr. Smith danced a furious step and so the drums went mad. The over-zealous converts who had smarted under Mr. Brown's restraining hand now flourished in full favor. One of them was Enoch, the son of the snake-priest who was believed to have killed and eaten the sacred python. Enoch's devotion to the new faith had seemed so much greater than Mr. Brown's that the villagers called him the outsider who wept louder than the bereaved.

Enoch was short and slight of build, and always seemed in great haste. His feet were short and broad, and when he stood or walked his heels came together and his feet opened outwards as if they had quarreled and meant to go in different directions. Such was the excessive energy bottled up in Enoch's small body that it was always erupting in quarrels and fights. On Sundays he always imagined that the sermon was preached for the benefit of his enemies. And if he happened to sit near one of them he would occasionally turn to give him a meaningful look, as if to say, 'I told you so.' It was Enoch who touched off the great conflict between church and clan in Umuofia which had been gathering since Mr. Brown left.

It happened during the annual ceremony which

was held in honor of the earth deity. At such times the ancestors of the clan who had been committed to Mother Earth at their death emerged again as *egwugwu* through tiny ant-holes.

One of the greatest crimes a man could commit was to unmask an *egwugwu* in public, or to say or do anything which might reduce its immortal prestige in the eyes of the uninitiated. And this was what Enoch did.

The annual worship of the earth goddess fell on a Sunday, and the masked spirits were abroad. The Christian women who had been to church could not therefore go home. Some of their men had gone out to beg the *egwugwu* to retire for a short while for the women to pass. They agreed and were already retiring, when Enoch boasted aloud that they would not dare to touch a Christian. Whereupon they all came back and one of them gave Enoch a good stroke of the cane, which was always carried. Enoch fell on him and tore off his mask. The other *egwugwu* immediately surrounded their desecrated companion, to shield him from the profane gaze of women and children, and led him away. Enoch had killed an ancestral spirit, and Umuofia was thrown into confusion.

That night the Mother of the Spirits walked the length and breadth of the clan, weeping for her murdered son. It was a terrible night. Not even the oldest man in Umuofia had ever heard such a strange and fearful sound, and it was never to be heard again. It seemed as if the very soul of the tribe wept for a great evil that was coming – its own death.

On the next day all the masked *egwugwu* of Umuofia assembled in the market place. They came from all the quarters of the clan and even from the neighboring villages. The dreaded Otakagu came from Imo, and Ekwensu, dangling a white cock, arrived from Uli. It was a terrible gathering. The eerie voices of countless spirits, the bells that clattered behind some of them, and the clash of machetes as they ran forwards and backwards and saluted one another, sent tremors of fear into every heart. For the first time in living memory the sacred bull-roarer was heard in broad daylight.

From the market place the furious band made for Enoch's compound. Some of the elders of the clan went with them, wearing heavy protections of charms and amulets. These were men whose arms were strong in *ogwu*, or medicine. As for the ordinary men and women, they listened from the safety of their huts.

The leaders of the Christians had met together at Mr. Smith's parsonage on the previous night. As they deliberated they could hear the Mother of Spirits wailing for her son. The chilling sound affected Mr. Smith, and for the first time he seemed to be afraid.

'What are they planning to do?' he asked. No one knew, because such a thing had never happened before. Mr. Smith would have sent for the District Commissioner and his court messengers, but they had gone on tour on the previous day.

'One thing is clear,' said Mr. Smith. 'We cannot offer physical resistance to them. Our strength lies in the Lord.' They knelt down together and prayed to God for delivery.

'O Lord, save Thy people,' cried Mr. Smith.

'And bless Thine inheritance,' replied the men.

They decided that Enoch should be hidden in the parsonage for a day or two. Enoch himself was greatly disappointed when he heard this, for he had hoped that a holy war was imminent; and there were a few other Christians who thought like him. But wisdom prevailed in the camp of the faithful and many lives were thus saved.

The band of *egwugwu* moved like a furious whirl-wind to Enoch's compound and with machete and fire reduced it to a desolate heap. And from there they made for the church, intoxicated with destruction.

Mr. Smith was in his church when he heard the masked spirits coming. He walked quietly to the door which commanded the approach to the church compound, and stood there. But when the first three or four *egwugwu* appeared on the church compound he nearly bolted. He overcame this impulse and instead of running away he went down the two steps that led up to the church and walked towards the approaching spirits.

They surged forward, and a long stretch of the bamboo fence with which the church compound was surrounded gave way before them. Discordant bells clanged, machetes clashed and the air was full of dust and weird sounds. Mr. Smith heard a sound of foot-steps behind him. He turned round and saw Okeke, his interpreter. Okeke had not been on the best of terms with his master since he had strongly con-demned Enoch's behavior at the meeting of the leaders of the church during the night. Okeke had gone as far as to say that Enoch should not be hidden in the parsonage, because he would only draw the wrath of the clan on the pastor. Mr. Smith had re-buked him in very strong language, and had not sought his advice that morning. But now, as he came up and stood by him confronting the angry spirits, Mr. Smith looked at him and smiled. It was a wan smile, but there was deep gratitude there.

For a brief moment the onrush of the *egwugwu* was checked by the unexpected composure of the two men. But it was only a momentary check, like the tense silence between blasts of thunder. The second onrush was greater than the first. It swallowed up the two men. Then an unmistakable voice rose above the tumult and there was immediate silence. Space was made around the two men, and Ajofia began to speak.

Ajofia was the leading *egwugwu* of Umuofia. He was the head and spokesman of the nine ancestors who administered justice in the clan. His voice was unmistakable and so he was able to bring immediate peace to the agitated spirits. He then addressed Mr. Smith, and as he spoke clouds of smoke rose from his head.

'The body of the white man, I salute you,' he said, using the language in which immortals spoke to men.

'The body of the white man, do you know me?' he asked.

Mr. Smith looked at his interpreter, but Okeke, who was a native of distant Umuru, was also at a loss.

Ajofia laughed in his guttural voice. It was like the laugh of rusty metal. 'They are strangers,' he said, 'and they are ignorant. But let that pass.' He turned round to his comrades and saluted them, calling them the fathers of Umuofia. He dug his rattling spear into the ground and it shook with metallic life. Then he turned once more to the missionary and his interpreter.

'Tell the white man that we will not do him any harm,' he said to the interpreter. 'Tell him to go back to his house and leave us alone. We liked his brother who was with us before. He was foolish, but we liked him, and for his sake we shall not harm his brother. But this shrine which he built must be destroyed. We shall no longer allow it in our midst. It has bred untold abominations and we have come to put an end to it.' He turned to his comrades. 'Fathers of Umuofia, I salute you;' and they replied with one guttural voice. He turned again to the missionary. 'You can stay with us if you like our ways. You can worship your own god. It is good that a man should worship the gods and the spirits of his fathers. Go back to your house so that you may not be hurt. Our anger is great but we have held it down so that we can talk to you.'

Mr. Smith said to his interpreter: 'Tell them to go away from here. This is the house of God and I will not live to see it desecrated.'

Okeke interpreted wisely to the spirits and leaders of Umuofia: 'The white man says he is happy you have come to him with your grievances, like friends. He will be happy if you leave the matter in his hands.'

'We cannot leave the matter in his hands because he does not understand our customs, just as we do not understand his. We say he is foolish because he does not know our ways, and perhaps he says we are foolish because we do not know his. Let him go away.'

Mr. Smith stood his ground. But he could not save his church. When the *egwugwu* went away the red-earth church which Mr. Brown had built was a pile of earth and ashes. And for the moment the spirit of the clan was pacified.

Twenty-three

FOR the first time in many years Okonkwo had a feeling that was akin to happiness. The times which had altered so unaccountably during his exile seemed to be coming round again. The clan which had turned false on him appeared to be making amends.

He had spoken violently to his clansmen when they had met in the market place to decide on their action. And they had listened to him with respect. It was like the good old days again, when a warrior was a warrior. Although they had not agreed to kill the missionary or drive away the Christians, they had agreed to do something substantial. And they had done it. Okonkwo was almost happy again.

For two days after the destruction of the church, nothing happened. Every man in Umuofia went about armed with a gun or a machete. They would not be caught unawares, like the men of Abame.

Then the District Commissioner returned from his tour. Mr. Smith went immediately to him and they had a long discussion. The men of Umuofia did not take any notice of this, and if they did, they thought it was not important. The missionary often went to see his brother white man. There was nothing strange in that.

Three days later the District Commissioner sent his sweet-tongued messenger to the leaders of Umuofia asking them to meet him in his headquarters. That also was not strange. He often asked them to hold such palavers, as he called them. Okonkwo was among the six leaders he invited.

Okonkwo warned the others to be fully armed. 'An Umuofia man does not refuse a call,' he said. 'He may refuse to do what he is asked; he does not refuse to be asked. But the times have changed, and we must be fully prepared.'

And so the six men went to see the District Commissioner, armed with their machetes. They did not carry guns, for that would be unseemly. They were led into the courthouse where the District Commissioner sat. He received them politely. They unslung their goatskin bags and their sheathed machetes, put them on the floor, and sat down.

'I have asked you to come,' began the Commissioner, 'because of what happened during my absence. I have been told a few things but I cannot believe them until I have heard your own side. Let us talk about it like friends and find a way of ensuring that it does not happen again.'

Ogbuefi Ekwueme rose to his feet and began to tell the story.

'Wait a minute,' said the Commissioner. 'I want to bring in my men so that they too can hear your grievances and take warning. Many of them come from distant places and although they speak your tongue they are ignorant of your customs. James! Go and bring in the men.' His interpreter left the courtroom and soon returned with twelve men. They sat together with the men of Umuofia, and Ogbuefi Ekwueme began to tell the story of how Enoch murdered an *egwugwu*.

It happened so quickly that the six men did not see it coming. There was only a brief scuffle, too brief even to allow the drawing of a sheathed machete. The six men were handcuffed and led into the guardroom.

'We shall not do you any harm,' said the District Commissioner to them later, 'if only you agree to cooperate with us. We have brought a peaceful administration to you and your people so that you may be happy. If any man ill-treats you we shall come to your rescue. But we will not allow you to ill-treat others. We have a court of law where we judge cases and administer justice just as it is done in my own country under a great queen. I have brought you here because you joined together to molest others, to burn people's houses and their place of worship. That must not happen in the dominion of our queen, the most powerful ruler in the world. I have decided that you will pay a fine of two hundred bags of cowries. You will be released as soon as you agree to this and undertake to collect that fine from your people. What do you say to that?'

The six men remained sullen and silent and the Commissioner left them for a while. He told the court messengers, when he left the guardroom, to treat the men with respect because they were the leaders of Umuofia. They said, 'Yes, sir,' and saluted.

As soon as the District Commissioner left, the head messenger, who was also the prisoners' barber, took down his razor and shaved off all the hair on the men's heads. They were still handcuffed, and they just sat and moped.

'Who is the chief among you?' the court messengers asked in jest. 'We see that every pauper wears the anklet of title in Umuofia. Does it cost as much as ten cowries?'

The six men ate nothing throughout that day and the next. They were not even given any water to drink, and they could not go out to urinate or go into the bush when they were pressed. At night the messengers came in to taunt them and to knock their shaven heads together.

Even when the men were left alone they found no words to speak to one another. It was only on the third day, when they could no longer bear the hunger and the insults, that they began to talk about giving in.

'We should have killed the white man if you had listened to me,' Okonkwo snarled.

'We could have been in Umuru now waiting to be hanged,' someone said to him.

'Who wants to kill the white man?' asked a messenger who had just rushed in. Nobody spoke.

'You are not satisfied with your crime, but you must kill the white man on top of it.' He carried a strong stick, and he hit each man a few blows on the head and back. Okonkwo was choked with hate.

As soon as the six men were locked up, court messengers went into Umuofia to tell the people that their leaders would not be released unless they paid a fine of two hundred and fifty bags of cowries.

'Unless you pay the fine immediately,' said their head-man, 'we will take your leaders to Umuru before the big white man, and hang them.'

This story spread quickly through the villages, and was added to as it went. Some said that the men had already been taken to Umuru and would be hanged on the following day. Some said that their families would also be hanged. Others said that soldiers were already on their way to shoot the people of Umuofia as they had done in Abame.

It was the time of the full moon. But that night the voice of children was not heard. The village *ilo* where they always gathered for a moon-play was empty. The women of Iguedo did not meet in their secret enclosure to learn a new dance to be displayed later to the village. Young men who were always abroad in the moonlight kept their huts that night. Their manly voices were not heard on the village paths as they went to visit their friends and lovers. Umuofia was like a startled animal with ears erect, sniffing the silent, ominous air and not knowing which way to run.

The silence was broken by the village crier beating his sonorous *ogene*. He called every man in Umuofia, from the Akakanma age group upwards, to a meeting in the market place after the morning meal. He went from one end of the village to the other and walked all its breadth. He did not leave out any of the main footpaths.

Okonkwo's compound was like a deserted homestead. It was as if cold water had been poured on it. His family was all there, but everyone spoke in whispers. His daughter Ezinma had broken her twenty-eight day visit to the family of her future husband, and returned home when she heard that her father had been imprisoned, and was going to be hanged. As soon as she got home she went to Obierika to ask what the men of Umuofia were going to do about it. But Obierika had not been home since morning. His wives thought he had gone to a secret meeting. Ezinma was satisfied that something was being done.

On the morning after the village crier's appeal the men of Umuofia met in the market place and decided to collect without delay two hundred and fifty bags of cowries to appease the white man. They did not know that fifty bags would go to the court messengers, who had increased the fine for that purpose.

Twenty-four

Oᴋᴏɴᴋᴡᴏ and his fellow prisoners were set free as soon as the fine was paid. The District Commissioner spoke to them again about the great queen, and about peace and good government. But the men did not listen. They just sat and looked at him and at his interpreter. In the end they were given back their bags and sheathed machetes and told to go home. They rose and left the courthouse. They neither spoke to anyone nor among themselves.

The courthouse, like the church, was built a little way outside the village. The footpath that linked them was a very busy one because it also led to the stream, beyond the court. It was open and sandy. Footpaths were open and sandy in the dry season. But when the rains came the bush grew thick on either side and closed in on the path. It was now dry season.

As they made their way to the village the six men met women and children going to the stream with their water-pots. But the men wore such heavy and fearsome looks that the women and children did not say '*nno*' or 'welcome' to them, but edged out of the way to let them pass. In the village little groups of men joined them until they became a sizable company. They walked silently. As each of the six men got to his compound, he turned in, taking some of the crowd with him. The village was astir in a silent, suppressed way.

Ezinma had prepared some food for her father as soon as news spread that the six men would be released. She took it to him in his *obi*. He ate absent-mindedly. He had no appetite; he only ate to please her. His male relations and friends had gathered in his *obi*, and Obierika was urging him to eat. Nobody else spoke, but they noticed the long stripes on Okonkwo's back where the warder's whip had cut into his flesh.

The village crier was abroad again in the night. He beat his iron gong and announced that another meeting would be held in the morning. Everyone knew that Umuofia was at last going to speak its mind about the things that were happening.

Okonkwo slept very little that night. The bitterness in his heart was now mixed with a kind of childlike excitement. Before he had gone to bed he had brought down his war dress, which he had not touched since his return from exile. He had shaken out his smoked raffia skirt and examined his tall feather head-gear and his shield. They were all satisfactory, he had thought.

As he lay on his bamboo bed he thought about the treatment he had received in the white man's court, and he swore vengeance. If Umuofia decided on war, all would be well. But if they chose to be cowards he would go out and avenge himself. He thought about wars in the past. The noblest, he thought, was the war against Isike. In those days Okudo was still alive. Okudo sang a war song in a way that no other man could. He was not a fighter, but his voice turned every man into a lion.

'Worthy men are no more,' Okonkwo sighed as he remembered those days. 'Isike will never forget how we slaughtered them in that war. We killed twelve of their men and they killed only two of ours. Before the end of the fourth market week they were suing for peace. Those were days when men were men.'

As he thought of these things he heard the sound of the iron gong in the distance. He listened carefully, and could just hear the crier's voice. But it was very faint. He turned on his bed and his back hurt him. He ground his teeth. The crier was drawing nearer and nearer until he passed by Okonkwo's compound.

'The greatest obstacle in Umuofia,' Okonkwo thought bitterly, 'is that coward, Egonwanne. His sweet tongue can change fire into cold ash. When he speaks he moves our men to impotence. If they had ignored his womanish wisdom five years ago, we would not have come to this.' He ground his teeth. 'Tomorrow he will tell them that our fathers never fought a "war of blame." If they listen to him I shall leave them and plan my own revenge.'

The crier's voice had once more become faint, and the distance had taken the harsh edge off his iron gong. Okonkwo turned from one side to the other and derived a kind of pleasure from the pain his back gave him. 'Let Egonwanne talk about a "war of blame" tomorrow and I shall show him my back and head.' He ground his teeth.

The market place began to fill as soon as the sun rose. Obierika was waiting in his *obi* when Okonkwo came along and called him. He hung his goatskin bag and his sheathed machete on his shoulder and went out to join him. Obierika's hut was close to the road and he saw every man who passed to the market place. He had exchanged greetings with many who had already passed that morning.

When Okonkwo and Obierika got to the meeting place there were already so many people that if one threw up a grain of sand it would not find its way to the earth again. And many more people were coming from every quarter of the nine villages. It warmed Okonkwo's heart to see such strength of numbers. But he was looking for one man in particular, the man whose tongue he dreaded and despised so much.

'Can you see him?' he asked Obierika.

'Who?'

'Egonwanne,' he said, his eyes roving from one corner of the huge market place to the other. Most of the men sat on wooden stools they had brought with them.

'No,' said Obierika, casting his eyes over the crowd. 'Yes, there he is, under the silk-cotton tree. Are you afraid he would convince us not to fight?'

'Afraid? I do not care what he does to *you*. I despise him and those who listen to him. I shall fight alone if I choose.'

They spoke at the top of their voices because everybody was talking, and it was like the sound of a great market.

'I shall wait till he has spoken,' Okonkwo thought. 'Then I shall speak.'

'But how do you know he will speak against war?' Obierika asked after a while.

'Because I know he is a coward,' said Okonkwo. Obierika did not hear the rest of what he said because at that moment somebody touched his shoulder from behind and he turned round to shake hands and exchange greetings with five or six friends. Okonkwo did not turn round even though he knew the voices. He was in no mood to exchange greetings. But one of the men touched him and asked about the people of his compound.

'They are well,' he replied without interest.

The first man to speak to Umuofia that morning was Okika, one of the six who had been imprisoned.

Okika was a great man and an orator. But he did not have the booming voice which a first speaker must use to establish silence in the assembly of the clan. Onyeka had such a voice; and so he was asked to salute Umuofia before Okika began to speak.

'*Umuofia kwenu!*' he bellowed, raising his left arm and pushing the air with his open hand.

'*Yaa!*' roared Umuofia.

'*Umuofia kwenu!*' he bellowed again, and again and again, facing a new direction each time. And the crowd answered, '*Yaa!*'

There was immediate silence as though cold water had been poured on a roaring flame.

Okika sprang to his feet and also saluted his clansmen four times. Then he began to speak:

'You all know why we are here, when we ought to be building our barns or mending our huts, when we should be putting our compounds in order. My father used to say to me: "Whenever you see a toad jumping in broad daylight, then know that something is after its life." When I saw you all pouring into this meeting from all the quarters of our clan so early in the morning, I knew that something was after our life.' He paused for a brief moment and then began again:

'All our gods are weeping. Idemili is weeping, Ogwugwu is weeping, Agbala is weeping, and all the others. Our dead fathers are weeping because of the shameful sacrilege they are suffering and the abomination we have all seen with our eyes.' He stopped again to steady his trembling voice.

'This is a great gathering. No clan can boast of greater numbers or greater valor. But are we all here? I ask you: Are all the sons of Umuofia with us here?' A deep murmur swept through the crowd.

'They are not,' he said. 'They have broken the clan and gone their several ways. We who are here this morning have remained true to our fathers, but our brothers have deserted us and joined a stranger to soil their fatherland. If we fight the stranger we shall hit our brothers and perhaps shed the blood of a clansman. But we must do it. Our fathers never dreamed of such a thing, they never killed their brothers. But a white man never came to them. So we must do what our fathers would never have done. Eneke the bird was asked why he was always on the wing and he replied: "Men have learned to shoot without missing their mark and I have learned to fly without perching on a twig." We must root out this evil. And if our brothers take the side of evil we must root them out too. And we must do it *now*. We must bale this water now that it is only ankle-deep. . . .'

At this point there was a sudden stir in the crowd and every eye was turned in one direction. There was a sharp bend in the road that led from the market place to the white man's court, and to the stream beyond it. And so no one had seen the approach of the five court messengers until they had come round the bend, a few paces from the edge of the crowd. Okonkwo was sitting at the edge.

He sprang to his feet as soon as he saw who it was. He confronted the head messenger, trembling with hate, unable to utter a word. The man was fearless and stood his ground, his four men lined up behind him.

In that brief moment the world seemed to stand still, waiting. There was utter silence. The men of Umuofia were merged into the mute backcloth of trees and giant creepers, waiting.

The spell was broken by the head messenger. 'Let me pass!' he ordered.

'What do you want here?'

'The white man whose power you know too well has ordered this meeting to stop.'

In a flash Okonkwo drew his machete. The messenger crouched to avoid the blow. It was useless. Okonkwo's machete descended twice and the man's head lay beside his uniformed body.

The waiting backcloth jumped into tumultuous life and the meeting was stopped. Okonkwo stood looking at the dead man. He knew that Umuofia would not go to war. He knew because they had let the other messengers escape. They had broken into tumult instead of action. He discerned fright in that tumult. He heard voices asking: 'Why did he do it?'

He wiped his machete on the sand and went away.

Twenty-five

WHEN the District Commissioner arrived at Okonkwo's compound at the head of an armed band of soldiers and court messengers he found a small crowd of men sitting wearily in the *obi*. He commanded them to come outside, and they obeyed without a murmur.

'Which among you is called Okonkwo?' he asked through his interpreter.

'He is not here,' replied Obierika.

'Where is he?'

'He is not here!'

The Commissioner became angry and red in the face. He warned the men that unless they produced Okonkwo forthwith he would lock them all up. The men murmured among themselves, and Obierika spoke again.

'We can take you where he is, and perhaps your men will help us.'

The Commissioner did not understand what Obierika meant when he said, 'Perhaps your men will help us.' One of the most infuriating habits of these people was their love of superfluous words, he thought.

Obierika with five or six others led the way. The Commissioner and his men followed, their firearms held at the ready. He had warned Obierika that if he and his men played any monkey tricks they would be shot. And so they went.

There was a small bush behind Okonkwo's compound. The only opening into this bush from the compound was a little round hole in the red-earth wall through which fowls went in and out in their endless search for food. The hole would not let a man through. It was to this bush that Obierika led the Commissioner and his men. They skirted round the compound, keeping close to the wall. The only sound they made was with their feet as they crushed dry leaves.

Then they came to the tree from which Okonkwo's body was dangling, and they stopped dead.

'Perhaps your men can help us bring him down and bury him,' said Obierika. 'We have sent for strangers from another village to do it for us, but they may be a long time coming.'

The District Commissioner changed instantaneous-ly. The resolute administrator in him gave way to the student of primitive customs.

'Why can't you take him down yourselves?' he asked.

'It is against our custom,' said one of the men. 'It is an abomination for a man to take his own life. It is an offense against the Earth, and a man who commits it will not be buried by his clansmen. His body is evil, and only strangers may touch it. That is why we ask your people to bring him down, because you are strangers.'

'Will you bury him like any other man?' asked the Commissioner.

'We cannot bury him. Only strangers can. We shall pay your men to do it. When he has been buried we will then do our duty by him. We shall make sacrifices to cleanse the desecrated land.'

Obierika, who had been gazing steadily at his friend's dangling body, turned suddenly to the District Commissioner and said ferociously: 'That man was one of the greatest men in Umuofia. You drove him to kill himself; and now he will be buried like a dog. . . .' He could not say any more. His voice trembled and choked his words.

'Shut up!' shouted one of the messengers, quite unnecessarily.

'Take down the body,' the Commissioner ordered his chief messenger, 'and bring it and all these people to the court.'

'Yes, sah,' the messenger said, saluting.

The Commissioner went away, taking three or four of the soldiers with him. In the many years in which he had toiled to bring civilization to different parts of Africa he had learned a number of things. One of them was that a District Commissioner must never attend to such undignified details as cutting a hanged man from the tree. Such attention would give the natives a poor opinion of him. In the book which he planned to write he would stress that point. As he walked back to the court he thought about that book. Every day brought him some new material. The story of this man who had killed a messenger and hanged himself would make interesting reading. One could almost write a whole chapter on him. Perhaps not a whole chapter but a reasonable paragraph, at any rate. There was so much else to include, and one must be firm in cutting out details. He had already chosen the title of the book, after much thought: *The Pacification of the Primitive Tribes of the Lower Niger.*

A GLOSSARY OF IBO WORDS AND PHRASES

agadi-nwayi: old woman.

agbala: woman; also used of a man who has taken no title.

chi: personal god.

efulefu: worthless man.

egwugwu: a masquerader who impersonates one of the ancestral spirits of the village.

ekwe: a musical instrument; a type of drum made from wood.

eneke-nti-oba: a kind of bird.

eze-agadi-nwayi: the teeth of an old woman.

iba: fever.

ilo: the village green, where assemblies for sports, discussions, etc., take place.

inyanga: showing off, bragging.

isa-ifi: a ceremony. If a wife had been separated from her husband for some time and were then to be re-united with him, this ceremony would be held to ascertain that she had not been unfaithful to him during the time of their separation.

iyi-uwa: a special kind of stone which forms the link between an *ogbanje* and the spirit world. Only if the *iyi-uwa* were discovered and destroyed would the child not die.

jigida: a string of waist-beads.

kotma: court messenger. The word is not of Ibo origin but is a corruption of 'court messenger.'

kwenu: a shout of approval and greeting.

ndichie: elders.

nna ayi: our father.

nno: welcome.

nso-ani: a religious offense of a kind abhorred by everyone, literally earth's taboo.

nza: a very small bird.

obi: the large living quarters of the head of the family.

obodo dike: the land of the brave.

ochu: murder or manslaughter.

ogbanje: a changeling; a child who repeatedly dies and returns to its mother to be reborn. It is almost impossible to bring up an *ogbanje* child without it dying, unless its *iyi-uwa* is first found and destroyed.

ogene: a musical instrument; a kind of gong.

oji odu achu-ijiji-o: cow. (i.e., the one that uses its tail to drive flies away.)

osu: outcast. Having been dedicated to a god, the *osu* was taboo and was not allowed to mix with the freeborn in any way.

Oye: the name of one of the four market days.

ozo: the name of one of the titles or ranks.

tufia: a curse or oath.

udu: a musical instrument; a type of drum made from pottery.

uli: a dye used by women for drawing patterns on the skin.

umuada: a family gathering of daughters, for which the female kinsfolk return to their village of origin.

umunna: a wide group of kinsmen (the masculine form of the word *umuada*).

Uri: part of the betrothal ceremony when the dowry is paid.

CONNECTIONS

The Second Coming

William Butler Yeats

Turning and turning in the widening gyre
The falcon cannot hear the falconer;
Things fall apart; the centre cannot hold;
Mere anarchy is loosed upon the world,
The blood-dimmed tide is loosed, and everywhere
The ceremony of innocence is drowned;
The best lack all conviction, while the worst
Are full of passionate intensity.

Surely some revelation is at hand;
Surely the Second Coming is at hand.
The Second Coming! Hardly are those words out
When a vast image out of *Spiritus Mundi*[1]
Troubles my sight: somewhere in sands of the desert
A shape with lion body and the head of a man,
A gaze blank and pitiless as the sun,
Is moving its slow thighs, while all about it
Reel shadows of the indignant desert birds.
The darkness drops again; but now I know
That twenty centuries of stony sleep
Were vexed to nightmare by a rocking cradle,
And what rough beast, its hour come round at last,
Slouches towards Bethlehem to be born?

■ ■ ■

---

1. **Spiritus Mundi:** (Latin) spirit of the world

Conversations with Achebe

Nigerian Bard Tells His Own Story
Sonia Sanchez

It is not a small voice I heard when I entered his house situated on the Bard College campus at Annandale-on-Hudson, N.Y. This man Chinua Achebe. Born in Nigeria. Educated at Government College at Umuahia and finally at the University College in Ibadan. Since 1990, he has been Bard's Charles P. Stevenson Jr. professor of literature.

It is a voice that Gwendolyn Brooks, in a poem she wrote for him, says:

> . . . is committed to positives
> and to clarity.
> He writes in The Large.
> He is a master of imagery,
> of efficient music,
> Of working whimsy.
> He has not met you, but he
> knows you!
> Sometimes, attending him, you feel
> yourself
> Stayed by "ropes" of mean ice.
> He will say nothing that does
> not feel, and he
> will involve you in nothing
> beyond apprehension.

It is this "large" voice that I heard recently on a Saturday morning, moving out of Africa into the world with rhythms, idioms and proverbs of Igbo culture.

Things Fall Apart is a novel set in Igbo country in the middle of the 19th Century. It tells a story of traditional village life in Africa before the invasion of Europeans and the destruction of that life with the introduction of Christianity, missionaries, and petty functionaries.

SANCHEZ: Tell me about the genesis of *Things Fall Apart*.

ACHEBE: What I was trying to say, put quite simply, is that when I began writing, I was only conscious of the fact that my story had not been told. You see, I had read many stories. I had gone to the university, and I had read stories, fiction, and poetry supposedly about me, and I could never recognize myself in these stories. I knew that my story was missing.

And the stories told about me by others, I could not accept because I lacked dignity [in them]. These people did not give me dignity, and I knew I had it. So it was necessary for me to tell my own story.

SANCHEZ: As I reread the novel for this interview, I felt again that your protagonist, Okonkwo, was fated to fail, fated to move in constant fear and anger, fated to end hanging from a morning sky of death. Was that because Okonkwo had a bad *chi?*

ACHEBE: Well, the Igbo people believe that we have our own personal *chi,* and they do talk about a good *chi* and a bad *chi.* But it's only a metaphorical way of talking, because logically, *chi* is a little fragment of the essence of God. So what people mean when they say I have a bad *chi,* they mean I have bad luck.

It's a very complex way of looking at the world. It's not simply something outside of you that is responsible for your lack of success or lack of achievement or whatever it is that you are looking for. Perhaps you yourself have not done all that you should have done. They are anxious not to put it all on your *chi.*

But you, of course, being human, want to put it on somebody else. The Igbo people are . . . trying to say, "Yes, it is this, but it is also that," so that you know life is not simple.

I wouldn't say that for Okonkwo there is no way out. The cards were stacked against him. I mean, his father, Unoka, was not successful, so Okonkwo had this fear in him that he was actually his father's son and that was what scared him. That is why he was fighting so relentlessly to kill that possibility of his father resurfacing in him.

Whether you call it genes or fate, he knew he was this man's son and he wanted to be as different from his father as he could be. So he exaggerated everything. He heard the loud sounds: bravery, success, wisdom, strength, but not compassion. He failed to hear the subtle admonition of his culture, which is that it's wonderful to be brave, but remember also that the coward outlives the brave man.

SANCHEZ: At what point do your characters take over from you when you are writing?

ACHEBE: They take over very early. I mean, the novel is not working when you are in control all the way through. It is working when these characters become people and you have drawn the parameters of the course.

But if they are really going to live and move at what they are being within the novel, they become autonomous and you are no longer to order them around.

SANCHEZ: When you wrote *Things Fall Apart,* it was posited at the turn of the 19th century. Is *Things Fall Apart* still relevant to us now at the beginning of the 21st century?

ACHEBE: A whole crop of leaders were created who were reared in the belief that they didn't have to care. We are in the hands of leaders who were reared in the colonial belief that the ruler doesn't have to be responsible to his people. *Things Fall Apart* tells us how it happened.

And I remember what Jimmy Baldwin said about my protagonist, Okonkwo. He said, "That man is my father. Yes," he said. "I don't know how he got over here but he did." And we who watched television in Africa would say that Black man is African.

SANCHEZ: Are you optimistic about Nigeria?

ACHEBE: Well, I'm not optimistic, but I'm not pessimistic, either. I simply think that we have a difficult job to do in my country and the reason that the military is behaving the way it's behaving is that we have not—we the civilians—allowed principles to rule our conduct. It's the opportunism of one group seeking the advantage over the other.

When we learn to deal with this, then the military will go. And we will begin our difficult march, because it's always going to be difficult. This legacy of colonial rule that we spoke about is not something we can just shake off one morning and say now it's over. There are many things we must unlearn and learn how to be free.

SANCHEZ: What role would the artist play in this?

ACHEBE: An essential role, because the artist is dealing with the most vital element of the people's condition, that which is called the human condition. The artist is one who looks at this closely and carefully and without apology and without condescension; he doesn't put anybody down. He's not owned by anybody, either. He looks at our condition as it is.

Interview published in March, 1995.

An Interview With Chinua Achebe

Patrick H. Samway

Could you trace for me some of the early steps in your life that led to writing fiction as a career?

I was born in the village of Ogidi in eastern Nigeria, which is close to the large market of Onitsha, in 1930. In those days there was considerable missionary activity in this area. First came the Anglicans and then the Roman Catholics. My father, who graduated from a teachers' college in

1904, was an early convert to Christianity in my village. I was born the second-to-the-last of my parents' six living children. My father retired from teaching in 1935 and returned to Ogidi; he had spent about 35 years working for the Church Missionary Society in Nigeria. As a missionary family, we went to church regularly and read the Bible a good deal; but there was also another part of the village that was not Christian (one of my father's brothers, in fact, was not Christian). So in my early years, I was exposed to both the Christian faith and the traditional religion of the Ibo people. When I look back, what was important to me then was that I was exposed to two different ways of seeing the world. Without knowing it, I was fascinated by the interplay between them.

I went to a Church Missionary Society primary school and then to one of the colleges [high school] established by the Nigerian Government, which was modeled on the English system. One advantage to this system was that there was a good library. We read a good deal, especially those books that one would normally read in a British school, such as *Treasure Island* and *Mill on the Floss*. I also read, though they were not labeled as such, books about Africa; most were simple stories about good white people and sinister savages. Then I was not really old enough to recognize what was going on, but, with hindsight, it was when I realized the implications of these stories that I finally came to the conclusion that something had to be done. New stories had to be written; those of the white man and the savage were really not my story. And thus the genesis of my desire to tell my own story and the story of my people. Later, when I went to the University of Nigeria at Ibadan, I made a conscious decision actually to start writing.

In mid-April of this year, I saw in Lagos a fine dramatic production of your novel Things Fall Apart, *adapted for the stage by Bassey Effiong for Diamond Productions, a relatively new theater outfit committed to encouraging drama in English in Nigeria. In this play, I was particularly impressed by the staging of the death of Okonkwo, the protagonist; it was like a self-crucifixion for having bucked the inroads made by the missionaries. How has the character of Okonkwo grown with you over the years?*

Okonkwo is very much part of my life and, as you say, of my development over the years. I thought about him for a long time before I knew I was going to write a novel. The side-by-side existence of Christianity and Ibo traditional religion was always in my mind. The story of Okonkwo is almost inevitable; if I hadn't written about him, certainly someone else would have, because it really is the beginning of our story. It is not all of it, but it is the beginning. I knew that I should construct a straightforward story that would not have, for example, the multiple dimensions of what later came about in *Arrow of God*.

Things Fall Apart needed a main character who saw things in terms of either/or and thought he was a defender of his own culture. And he was. The only problem is that the world was more complex than Okonkwo understood. Of course, this is the substance of tragedy.

Okonkwo feels very strongly that he is fighting for a cause, and yet that cause is not fully understood by him because Ibo life and culture say that one must be strong, and yet weakness is important. We must respect and prepare for weakness. We have a proverb that says that you can stand in the house of a coward and point to where a brave man once stood. The strong man has been destroyed by his bravery. The story of Okonkwo is in a way the story of our culture; he pays a price because he places too much emphasis on strength and manliness. Not enough attention is given to those who are oppressed. Okonkwo stands as a symbol of that price that must be paid.

I must say that, in addition to Okonkwo, Ezeulu in Arrow of God *is one of my favorite characters in your fiction. Where is Ezeulu situated in your creative world?*

I think Ezeulu is important because he brings in that dimension of complexity without which our understanding of human life is very superficial. He also introduces into my fiction the element of the divine. No matter what arrangements we make, there are times when we are not in control of our

lives. Some critics see the situation of Ezeulu in a
too-simple way ("He is an arrogant man who
wants to exercise power") and they never go
beyond this. Indeed he is self-willed and vindic-
tive, but he is more than that: He is a traditional
priest. He does not willingly falsify the wishes
of his gods. He conscientiously upholds his traditional beliefs, and if he comes to a "sticky" end, it
is just the nature of our world and our humanity.
Okonkwo would not listen to the other side;
Ezeulu, on the other hand, is ready to listen to the
other side in the persons of T. K. Winterbottom
and Tony Clarke, provided his dignity is not
insulted. Yet, he doesn't fare any better in the
end than Okonkwo. It is a different type of
Nigerian tragedy, but tragic nevertheless.

*What are the advantages and disadvantages
of writing and teaching in English and not in Ibo,
Yoruba or Hausa, or in any of the other 200-plus
languages in Nigeria?*

We will never forget that English is a language imposed on us. Over the years, English
became the "dominant" language in certain ways,
precisely because of the British presence among
us. The British, in fact, created the entity now
called Nigeria; they put together an area compris-
ing many nations and peoples and imposed their
colonial rule. When modern education began, it
also followed the British way. We could have said
in 1960, when the British left Nigeria, that we
wanted to fashion something to follow it. But we

have not taken that rather drastic step. What we have is not perfect, but the problems of trying to unscramble all this would be even greater. So we said and continue to say in effect, "Let this nation we now call Nigeria move on to other things." Today we would not be able to govern the country called Nigeria without English.

Some think that because I write in English, more people outside Nigeria than within the country read my books. This is not the case: Seventy-five percent of the sales of my books are in Nigeria. Though a foreign language, English has been in Nigeria for 100 years. My use of English is mainly based on practical considerations, not on ideological ones. You should know that I write at times in Ibo, particularly poetry and children's stories, and I find that as rewarding as the work I do in English. I consider myself to be bilingual. Though we transact our business in English, we need to make sure, at the same time, that the indigenous languages of Nigeria survive and grow. And those who use various native languages and dialects have the responsibility to keep them alive. Neither official legislation nor statutes can do this; that only creates havoc as it has done in India, for example. Every writer has to decide which language he or she wishes to write in. We must be very patient when it comes to legislating anything concerning language.

On March 22, 1990, you were involved in a serious car accident on the highway between

Nsukka and Onitsha and subsequently spent six months in England undergoing operations and therapy before coming to the United States. How do you see your life changing as a result of this accident?

I came very, very close to death. In fact, the U.S. doctors did not believe that I survived this accident when they looked at my initial X-rays. But since I didn't die, it means that I must continue my work. My fundamental conviction is that I need to do what I can in the time that is left. I have been privileged to receive a post at Bard and to be touched by many inside and outside Nigeria who have written saying how they appreciate my work. I am terribly moved by all this. The nature of my writing might change by what I have undergone, but I cannot predict exactly what will happen. I plan to continue with a novel I have in mind, but I am not sure how the details will develop. In addition, I hope to write my autobiography in the near future because so much has happened to me in the recent past. So, you see, my days will be full.

Interview conducted on June 12, 1991.

■ ■ ■

The Indian's Night Promises to Be Dark

Chief Seattle

The experience of white colonists stretching into the far reaches of a continent is not unique to Africa. In North America, white settlers moved into the lands of the native people of the Pacific Northwest, and by 1853 they were followed by the U.S. government. That year, the Washington Territory was established and the town of Seattle was laid out. In 1855, the American Indian Seattle, chief of the Suquamish and Duwamish peoples and the man for whom the town was named, signed a treaty with the first territorial governor, Isaac Stevens.

At some point between the founding of the territory and the signing of the treaty, a public meeting between Seattle and Stevens is said to have occurred. According to the only existing account of the meeting, that of Dr. Henry Smith, the governor first delivered an address. Then Seattle rose up and spoke. His speech was translated into English, and Smith took notes. Smith used those notes to reconstruct Seattle's speech, which was published in the Seattle Sunday Star *in October of 1887. This article is the only evidence that the meeting took place, and one badly damaged copy of that newspaper is all that now remains. The text that follows is Smith's 1887 reconstruction. Where the* Seattle Sunday Star *is no longer readable, words and phrases have been taken from an 1891 reprinting.*

Yonder sky that has wept tears of compassion on our fathers for centuries untold, and which, to us, looks eternal, may change. Today it is fair, tomorrow it may be overcast with clouds. My words are like the stars that never set. What Seattle says, the great chief, Washington, can rely upon, with as much certainty as our pale-face brothers can rely upon the return of the seasons.

The son of the white chief says his father sends us greetings of friendship and good will. This is kind, for we know he has little need of our friendship in return, because his people are many. They are like the grass that covers the vast prairies, while my people are few, and resemble the scattering trees of a storm-swept plain.

The great, and I presume also good, white chief sends us word that he wants to buy our lands but is willing to allow us to reserve enough to live on comfortably. This indeed appears generous, for the red man no longer has rights that he need respect, and the offer may be wise, also, for we are no longer in need of a great country.

There was a time when our people covered the whole land, as the waves of a wind-ruffled sea cover its shell-paved floor. But that time has long since passed away with the greatness of tribes now almost forgotten. I will not mourn over our untimely decay, nor reproach my pale-face brothers for hastening it, for we, too, may have been somewhat to blame.

When our young men grow angry at some real or imaginary wrong, and disfigure their faces with black paint, their hearts, also, are disfigured and turn black, and then their cruelty is relentless and knows no bounds, and our old men are not able to restrain them.

But let us hope that hostilities between the red-man and his pale-face brothers may never return. We would have everything to lose and nothing to gain.

True it is, that revenge, with our young braves, is considered gain, even at the cost of their own lives, but old men who stay at home in times of war, and old women, who have sons to lose, know better.

Our great father Washington, for I presume he is now our father, as well as yours, since George has moved his boundaries to the north; our great and good father, I say, sends us word by his son, who, no doubt, is a great chief among his people, that if we do as he desires, he will protect us. His brave armies will be to us a bristling wall of strength, and his great ships of war will fill our harbors so that our ancient enemies far to the north-ward, the Simsiams and Hydas, will no longer frighten our women and old men. Then he will be our father and we will be his children.

But can this ever be?

Your God loves your people and hates mine; he folds his strong arms lovingly around the white man and leads him as a father leads his infant son, but he has forsaken his red children; he makes your people wax strong every day, and soon they will fill the land; while my people are ebbing away like a fast-receding tide, that will never flow again. The white man's God cannot love his red children or he would protect them. They seem to be orphans and can look nowhere for help. How then can we become brothers? How can your father become our father and bring us prosperity and awaken in us dreams of returning greatness?

Your God seems to us to be partial. He came to the white man. We never saw Him; never even heard His voice; He gave the white man laws but He had no word for His red children whose teeming millions filled this vast continent as the stars fill the firmament. No, we are two distinct races and must ever remain so. There is little in common between us. The ashes of our ancestors are sacred and their final resting place is hallowed ground, while you wander away from the tombs of your fathers seemingly without regret.

Your religion was written on tables of stone by the iron finger of an angry God, lest you might forget it. The red man could never remember nor comprehend it.

Our religion is the traditions of our ancestors, the dreams of our old men, given them by the great Spirit, and the visions of our sachems, and is written in the hearts of our people.

Your dead cease to love you and the homes of their nativity as soon as they pass the portals of the tomb. They wander far off beyond the stars, are soon forgotten, and never return. Our dead never forget the beautiful world that gave them being. They still love its winding rivers, its great mountains and its sequestered vales, and they ever yearn in tenderest affection over the lonely hearted living and often return to visit and comfort them.

Day and night cannot dwell together. The red man has ever fled the approach of the white man, as the changing mists on the mountain side flee before the blazing morning sun.

However, your proposition seems a just one, and I think my folks will accept it and will retire to the reservation you offer them, and we will dwell apart and in peace, for the words of the great white chief seem to be the voice of nature speaking to my people out of the thick darkness that is fast gathering around them like a dense fog floating inward from a midnight sea.

It matters but little where we pass the remainder of our days. They are not many.

The Indian's night promises to be dark. No bright star hovers about the horizon. Sad-voiced winds moan in the distance. Some grim Nemesis of our race is on the red man's trail, and wherever he goes he will still hear the sure approaching footsteps of the fell destroyer and prepare to meet his doom, as does the wounded doe that hears the approaching footsteps of the hunter. A few more moons, a few more winters, and not one of all the mighty hosts that once filled this broad land or that now roam in fragmentary bands through these vast solitudes will remain to weep over the tombs of a people once as powerful and hopeful as your own.

But why should we repine? Why should I murmur at the fate of my people? Tribes are made up of individuals and are no better than they. Men come and go like the waves of the sea. A tear, a tamanawus, a dirge, and they are gone from our longing eyes forever. Even the white man, whose God walked and talked with him, as friend to friend, is not exempt from the common destiny. We *may* be brothers after all. We shall see.

We will ponder your proposition, and when we have decided we will tell you. But should we accept it, I here and now make this the first condition: That we not be denied the privilege, without molestation, of visiting at will the graves of our ancestors and friends. Every part of this country is sacred to my people. Every hill-side, every valley, every plain and grove has been hallowed by some fond memory or some sad experience of my tribe.

Even the rocks that seem to lie dumb as they swelter in the sun along the silent seashore in solemn grandeur thrill with memories of past events connected with the fate of my people, and the very dust under your feet responds more lovingly to our footsteps than to yours, because it is the ashes of our ancestors, and our bare feet are conscious of the sympathetic touch, for the soil is rich with the life of our kindred.

The sable braves, and fond mothers, and glad-hearted maidens, and the little children who lived and rejoiced here, and whose very names are now forgotten, still love these solitudes, and their deep fastnesses at eventide grow shadowy with the presence of dusky spirits. And when the last red man shall have perished from the earth and his memory among white men shall have become a myth, these shores shall swarm with the invisible dead of my tribe, and when your children's children shall think themselves alone in the field, the store, the shop, upon the highway or in the silence of the woods they will not be alone. In all the earth there is no place dedicated to solitude. At night, when the streets of your cities and villages shall be silent, and you think them deserted, they will throng with the returning hosts that once filled and still love this beautiful land. The white man will never be alone. Let him be just and deal kindly with my people, for the dead are not altogether powerless.

■ ■ ■

•••

The Jungle Commission

Jomo Kenyatta

The relation between the Gikuyu and the Europeans can well be illustrated by a Gikuyu story which says: That once upon a time an elephant made a friendship with a man. One day a heavy thunderstorm broke out, the elephant went to his friend, who had a little hut at the edge of the forest, and said to him: "My dear good man, will you please let me put my trunk inside your hut to keep it out of this torrential rain?" The man, seeing what situation his friend was in, replied: "My dear good elephant, my hut is very small, but there is room for your trunk and myself. Please put your trunk in gently." The elephant thanked his friend, saying: "You have done me a good deed and one day I shall return your kindness." But what followed? As soon as the elephant put his trunk inside the hut, slowly he pushed his head inside, and finally flung the man out in the rain, and then lay down comfortably inside his friend's hut, saying: "My dear good friend, your skin is harder than mine, and as there is not enough room for both of us, you can afford to remain in the rain while I am protecting my delicate skin from the hailstorm."

The man, seeing what his friend had done to him, started to grumble; the animals in the nearby forest heard the noise and came to see what was the matter. All stood around listening to the heated argument between the man and his friend the elephant.

In this turmoil the lion came along roaring, and said in a loud voice: "Don't you all know that I am the King of the Jungle! How dare anyone disturb the peace of my kingdom?" On hearing this the elephant, who was one of the high ministers in the jungle kingdom, replied in a soothing voice, and said: "My Lord, there is no disturbance of the peace in your kingdom. I have only been having a little discussion with my friend here as to the possession of this little hut which your lordship sees me occupying." The lion, who wanted to have "peace and tranquillity" in his kingdom, replied in a noble voice, saying: "I command my ministers to appoint a Commission of Enquiry to go thoroughly into this matter and report accordingly." He then turned to the man and said: "You have done well by establishing friendship with my people, especially with the elephant who is one of my honourable ministers of state. Do not grumble any more, your hut is not lost to you. Wait until the sitting of my Imperial Commission, and there you will be given plenty of opportunity to state your case. I am sure that you will be pleased with the findings of the Commission." The man was very pleased by these sweet words from the King of the Jungle, and innocently waited for his opportunity, in the belief that, naturally, the hut would be returned to him.

The elephant, obeying the command of his master, got busy with other ministers to appoint the Commission of Enquiry. The following elders of the jungle were appointed to sit in the Commission: (1) Mr. Rhinoceros; (2) Mr. Buffalo; (3) Mr. Alligator;

(4) The Rt. Hon. Mr. Fox to act as chairman; and
(5) Mr. Leopard to act as Secretary to the Commission.
On seeing the personnel, the man protested and
asked if it was not necessary to include in this
Commission a member from his side. But he was
told that it was impossible, since no one from his
side was well enough educated to understand the
intricacy of jungle law. Further, that there was nothing to fear, for the members of the Commission
were all men of repute for their impartiality in justice, and as they were gentlemen chosen by God
to look after the interests of races less adequately
endowed with teeth and claws, he might rest
assured that they would investigate the matter
with the greatest care and report impartially.

   The Commission sat to take the evidence. The
Rt. Hon. Mr. Elephant was first called. He came
along with a superior air, brushing his tusks with
a sapling which Mrs. Elephant had provided, and
in an authoritative voice said: "Gentlemen of the
Jungle, there is no need for me to waste your valuable time in relating a story which I am sure you all
know. I have always regarded it as my duty to protect the interests of my friends, and this appears to
have caused the misunderstanding between myself
and my friend here. He invited me to save his hut
from being blown away by a hurricane. As the hurricane had gained access owing to the unoccupied
space in the hut, I considered it necessary, in my
friend's own interests, to turn the undeveloped
space to a more economic use by sitting in it myself; a duty which any of you would undoubtedly

have performed with equal readiness in similar circumstances."

After hearing the Rt. Hon. Mr. Elephant's conclusive evidence, the Commission called Mr. Hyena and other elders of the jungle, who all supported what Mr. Elephant had said. They then called the man, who began to give his own account of the dispute. But the Commission cut him short, saying: "My good man, please confine yourself to relevant issues. We have already heard the circumstances from various unbiased sources; all we wish you to tell us is whether the undeveloped space in your hut was occupied by anyone else before Mr. Elephant assumed his position?" The man began to say: "No, but—" But at this point the Commission declared that they had heard sufficient evidence from both sides and retired to consider their decision. After enjoying a delicious meal at the expense of the Rt. Hon. Mr. Elephant, they reached their verdict, called the man, and declared as follows: "In our opinion this dispute has arisen through a regrettable misunderstanding due to the backwardness of your ideas. We consider that Mr. Elephant has fulfilled his sacred duty of protecting your interests. As it is clearly for your good that the space should be put to its most economic use, and as you yourself have not yet reached the stage of expansion which would enable you to fill it, we consider it necessary to arrange a compromise to suit both parties. Mr. Elephant shall continue his occupation of your hut, but we give you permission to look for a site where you can build another hut more suited to your needs, and we will see that you are well protected."

The man, having no alternative, and fearing that his refusal might expose him to the teeth and claws of members of the Commission, did as they suggested. But no sooner had he built another hut than Mr. Rhinoceros charged in with his horn lowered and ordered the man to quit. A Royal Commission was again appointed to look into the matter, and the same finding was given. This procedure was repeated until Mr. Buffalo, Mr. Leopard, Mr. Hyena, and the rest were all accommodated with new huts. Then the man decided that he must adopt an effective method of protection, since Commissions of Enquiry did not seem to be of any use to him. He sat down and said: *"Ng'enda thi ndeagaga motegi,"* which literally means "there is nothing that treads on the earth that cannot be trapped," or in other words, you can fool people for a time, but not forever.

Early one morning, when the huts already occupied by the jungle lords were all beginning to decay and fall to pieces, he went out and built a bigger and better hut a little distance away. No sooner had Mr. Rhinoceros seen it than he came rushing in, only to find that Mr. Elephant was already inside, sound asleep. Mr. Leopard next came in at the window, Mr. Lion, Mr. Fox, and Mr. Buffalo entered the doors, while Mr. Hyena howled for a place in the shade and Mr. Alligator basked on the roof. Presently they all began disputing about their rights of penetration, and from disputing they came to fighting, and while they were all embroiled together the man set the hut on fire and burnt it to the ground, jungle lords and all. Then he went home, saying: "Peace is costly, but it's worth the expense," and lived happily ever after.

■   ■   ■

Ancient Wisdom
Uche Okeke

Okuku's Chickens

Mother Atulu, the sheep, and her little lambs were grazing out in an open field, when Nkwo, the kite[1], swooped down and made away with one lamb. Atulu stood open-mouthed. She did not so much as bleat once.

Nkwo was surprised by Mother Atulu's silence. "This mother's silence is very deep indeed. I do not like it so," he thought. He swooped down again and returned the young lamb to its mother.

A few days later, keen-eyed Nkwo sighted mother Okuku, the hen, and her chickens. He glided past in order to have a clearer view of them. Okuku noticed his sharply defined shadow and flapped her wings. Nkwo was encouraged.

Before Okuku knew it, one of her chickens was sky-bound. She squawked and fluttered her wings wildly. Nkwo watched the exercises with much pleasure. "This mother," he decided, "has fought her own fight. She must be tired and harmless!" He ate the chicken and from then on preyed on them.

---

1. **kite** (kīt): a bird with long, pointed wings and, usually, a forked tail that preys on insects, reptiles, and small mammals.

Old Sayings

A sun bird is king in its nest.

When a slogan reaches a small place, it becomes a great craze.

One who lets one's father's wealth waste away justifies one's self by saying that ripe palm nuts also waste away in the forest.

There are two knives in the home of the poor: The one that has a handle is not sharp; the other, that is sharp, has no handle.

A bird on the line dances, and the line dances with it.

One who toils for Ana, the earth goddess, should eat of the fruit of Ana.

An animal that imitates a monkey breaks its neck.

Extreme cleverness is madness.

The insane suffers shame, although not as much as his kith and kin.

The insane has as his companion his mind.

One who is undergoing a cure of hernia, who shows symptom of swelling of the belly, belongs to the evil forest.

The young of a kite cannot but fly.

One does not tire who runs for one's life.

A bird on a mound of earth is on the ground.

Let the kite perch, let the eagle perch. The one that bars the other, let its wings break.

One who is surrounded by one's enemies is always on the alert.

Where fire burns out, there the ashes remain.

Instruct the clever and he wears a cloth; instruct the fool and he wears a sword!

The snail moves with its shell.

One does not tell a grown-up to get away from the sun.

The walk of the great annoys the dwarf.

■ ■ ■

The Garden of Evil

William Saidi

Mr. Parker said, *"WENA SKELEM, WENA,"*[1] speaking in kitchen kaffir[2].

Old Mwanza smiled his ancient smile. He surmised that Mr. Parker was complimenting him. His withered chest filled with pride. Mr. Parker was not generous with his praise. He was an inspector in the Northern Rhodesia Police.

"Ya, wena skelem wena Mwanza," Mr. Parker said again.

He was surveying with a lordly contentment the garden of vegetables. The dark rich greenness of the cabbages and the bright luscious greenness of the lettuce were mouth-watering. Everything exuded a health, a vitality and a delicious aliveness which rejuvenated Old Mwanza's tired faith in life.

Mr. Parker smiled at Old Mwanza. That too was a rarity and a bonus. Mr. Parker had false teeth. They were unnaturally almost obscenely white. To most Africans, they constituted an unfathomable curiosity, to be ogled at until the mystery was unraveled. Mr. Parker hated the experience.

Old Mwanza had discovered Mr. Parker's toothlessness on a day that was to prove portentous for both men.

---

1. "You are dangerous, you."
2. **kaffir** (kaf′ ər): 1. a member of any of several Bantu-speaking peoples in Southeast Africa. 2. In South Africa, a black African: a contemptuous term.

Mr. Parker's wife and three children had flown to Durban, Natal, in the Union of South Africa. They had gone for a weekend holiday with Mr. Parker's parents who lived there in the luxury of seaside retirement. Mr. Parker saw them off at Lusaka airport that morning and returned to the house with an evil, vengeful glint in his eye.

Mwanza worked steadily in the garden, wondering idly when his daughter would visit him from her home in Chilenje African township. Her last visit had been an elixir for Old Mwanza. She had brought her first-born child, two weeks old, his first grandchild. Old Mwanza gazed in lachrymose gratitude and amazement at the little cherubic face, its eyes closed softly and its fresh lips parted slightly. His daughter kept reminding him how much like him the little boy looked.

"Let your husband hear you say that and you will be sorry," he admonished her gently.

As he worked, with one ear cocked for outlandish noises from the huge house, he waited for the explosion. It was uncanny, he thought. Mr. Parker's wife and children were away. The cook had taken the day off and so had the South African born nanny. Mr. Parker and Old Mwanza had the entire house and the vast garden and orchard to themselves. There was a tranquillity about the place, a tranquillity which Old Mwanza knew to be unnatural and transient.

It came two hours later.

"Mwanza, you skelem! Buya lapa! Buya lapa! You You bobojan!"[3]

He heard the shout clearly from behind the huge closed windows of the bedroom. Mr. Parker had a stentorian voice to match his police inspector's physique.

In his weak, reedy voice, Mwanza replied, *"Mina buya, Bwana!"*[4]

He could feel the tendons in his neck standing out with the exertion.

"Mina buya, Bwana!" He quickened his normally lugubrious, tortured pace. You are not a young man anymore and remember that stupid foot of yours, he reminded himself unnecessarily, as he hurried into the house.

In the bedroom, with its luxurious white furniture and expensive lace curtains, he found Mr. Parker lying cadaverously in the massive double bed with the snow-white eiderdown. His face was a bizarre study in drunken idiocy. The lips were slack and there were no teeth. The skin on the face was a flaming pink and the eyes appeared opaque and wild. Mr. Parker had no clothes on except a pair of white tennis shorts.

Old Mwanza walked fretfully into the room, his bare feet sinking dangerously into the thick pile of carpet. He waited. At last Mr. Parker stirred.

"Yes, *Bwana? Mina buyile.*"[5] Old Mwanza spoke in a tremulous whisper.

---

3. "Mwanza, you dangerous animal! Come here! You baboon!"
4. "I am coming, Master!"
5. "Yes, sir? I have come."

"Mwanza, *wena yazi lo skelem ena kona lapa township? Lapa Matelo, na lapa Chilenje? Wena yazi lo skelem? Ena fun bulala lo Mazungu, wena yazi? Ena funa bulala lo Mazungu.*[6] The stupid idiots!"

Old Mwanza had the weird sensation that this was a monologue. He kept his peace. Most white people in Northern Rhodesia spoke thus at this time. In Southern Rhodesia and Nyasaland, on the borders, the Africans were reported to be speaking of getting rid of the white people too. Mr. Parker had himself spoken like this before, even when he was sober. So Old Mwanza concluded benevolently that the viciousness came from the drink.

His discovery of Mr. Parker's toothlessness was a secret triumph for Old Mwanza. He was older and had all his teeth. It was true that he could not chew with the same efficiency as before, but he still had his teeth. Mr. Parker's misfortune (to Old Mwanza it was something to be utterly ashamed of, like losing your toes in a war) made him— Mr. Parker—vulnerable, mortal, weak and susceptible to all human frailties. For Old Mwanza, it was an astounding revelation.

Mr. Parker's speech had not been entirely shorn of its military thunder. Yet to Old Mwanza there was something comical about it. He concluded sagely that people with false teeth had no business trying to speak without them.

---

6. "Mwanza, you know those dangerous animals in Matero and Chilenje African townships? They want to kill all white people."

"Where are my teeth, Mwanza? *Upi lo* teeth *kamina? Upi Upi!*" Old Mwanza cast his tired eyes around the opulently furnished bedroom and wondered mischievously what would happen if the teeth, by some miracle, disappeared forever. His amusement was short-lived. The family had two cars and three servants, including the nanny, whom Old Mwanza had wooed in vain. The family always ate well, their dinner table invariably replete with fresh fruit, apart from the other victuals. To Old Mwanza, any European family which could afford fresh apples and oranges (not even from their own orchard) for dessert had to be rich.

The teeth were in a glass of water on a small table next to the bed. Old Mwanza cleared his throat to suppress laughter.

Loudly, he exclaimed dramatically, *"Bwana Bwana!"* with a shaking finger, he pointed to the glass, in which the dentures floated calmly.

Mr. Parker looked at the glass in amazement and laughed with exaggerated gusto, his rubbery lips stretched taut to reveal the barren pink gums in the darkened cave of his mouth. Old Mwanza felt laughter bubbling in his throat, but experience restrained him. To laugh with your master presumed equality. It could spell the end of a good job.

Mr. Parker walked regally along the smooth paths which separated the symmetrically arranged beds. Haughtily polite cauliflower looked with tolerant disdain at the lowly, peasant-looking cabbage. That perennial garden vegetable, the asparagus, looked with suspicion at the green virility of the spinach, while the juicy tomato, its eyes closed coyly, pleaded not to be bothered by the ungainly beet.

Old Mwanza thought Mr. Parker had at last begun to recognize the incredible beauty and aliveness of the garden. For years, he and the garden had lived a separate existence from the rest of the household. Even the cook, who marched neatly into the garden to cut vegetables for the pot, was an alien here. Mrs. Parker and the children? For all the attention they paid to the garden, it was nothing but a plaything for the eccentric, senile African gardener. It was Old Mwanza's kingdom, his own little garden of Eden. He knew every plant like the master of a castle knows his servants. Sometimes he would speak to them and a strange sensation would assail him, that they responded familiarly. Mr. Parker had not bought a hose or sprinkler for watering the garden. By tacit arrangement, Old Mwanza had devised his own ingenious irrigation system. This consisted of two cans fashioned crudely from two discarded four-gallon paraffin tins. These were suspended on a thick wooden pole placed horizontally on his shoulders. Old Mwanza did not know the pesticides by name. He could read or write after a fashion and only in his mother tongue, Nsenga, a derivative of the more widely spoken Nyamja of the

Eastern Province. He approached both writing and reading with acute trepidation and performed them only when his life or job depended on it.

Today, Mr. Parker walked in the garden as if he too wanted to be close to the plants. The prospect filled Old Mwanza with foreboding. He treasured his attachment to the garden to the point of being insanely possessive and jealous.

"There is no garden boy like you, my boy. You are . . . how old . . . about sixty? Yet, you are . . . you are just fantastic."

When Mr. Parker spoke to him in straight English, Old Mwanza felt humbled. It signified Mr. Parker's profound depth of feeling in what he was saying. That he believed that Old Mwanza had only a vague notion of what he was saying probably made him feel a martyr in the cause of better understanding between Europeans and Africans in the three troubled territories which constituted the ill-fated federation of Rhodesia and Nyasaland at the time.

Mr. Parker walked back into his house, leaving Old Mwanza to speculate anxiously on whether his daughter would visit him again. He lived in servants' quarters which were concealed from general view by a high wall between it and the big house. He had a bedroom and a kitchen to himself. The other half of the semidetached house was occupied by the cook, who was married.

Old Mwanza rarely ventured into the townships now. He had lived there all his life, raising his children with the same haphazard devotion that any other African paterfamilias raised their offspring in that detribalized maze.

During those sprightly days, Old Mwanza had worked as an office messenger, flitting from office building to office building on his bicycle, delivering letters, buying sandwiches and cold drinks and performing other menial errands for the Europeans. He enjoyed the social life too. Even his wife had enjoyed it, though she always went to the local church on Sundays. They lived in Matero, the African township on the outskirts of Lusaka. At weekends, he and his wife joined friends and neighbors in orgies of senseless drinking and singing. His wife recounted the events to the Catholic priest every Sunday. Old Mwanza became something of a local bon vivant until his wife clipped his wings. His ardor for the hedonistic life evaporated quite suddenly when she threatened to leave him unless he reformed. Abruptly, maturity came and without ever con-sciously acknowledging the fact, he recognized the essential truth that life did not finally consti-tute a series of liaisons with women of easy virtue. Then he joined friends who had boasted that there was adventure, fame and fortune to be made in the army. He went to Malaya and spent most of his time cooking. For all his relative security among the foul-smelling cabbages and beans, the Japanese had almost blown off his foot. It ended up with three toes, happily for Old

Mwanza, including the big one. When he returned, wiser but frightened of life, they gave him a medal and he gravitated almost inevitably to a night watchman's job. The foot gave him frightening moments and he changed to gardening. He had almost no hope and soon after his discovery that he and Nature wanted the same things he was more or less settled spiritually. His war experiences helped. They earned him the kind of respect that acted as a powerful talisman. He had fought on the side of RIGHT. In truth, he had only a hazy recollection of his days in the jungle of Malaya. After the Japanese had nearly blown off his foot, the whole experience became something of a living, waking nightmare.

As a gardener, he developed a liaison with Nature, an affinity which his first employer suspected had something to do with primitive witchcraft. In Mr. Parker's garden, Old Mwanza found his metier.

Often, he would sit up in bed, unable to sleep. Memories of his wife, memories of his halcyon days in Matero, memories of the cordite-filled days in Malaya would come flooding into his mind. His head would throb and reverberate and there would be explosions of a thousand cannons, their roar deafening. He would get up and walk into the quiet darkness of the night. In the distance he would hear the noise of barking dogs. In Chilenje township, they would be barking, not here in the European suburb of Woodlands,

where the dogs were trained to bark only when
there was an intruder. Mr. Parker had a basenji
dog, which Old Mwanza had been told never
barked. He had never heard it bark and had been
told by Mrs. Parker that the basenji was a rare
dog. It was so intelligent that it was almost
human, she said. It was probably the only one
of its kind in Northern Rhodesia, she claimed
breathlessly. Old Mwanza, who had been raised
entirely in the city where respect for dogs was
only incidental, did not believe her. A dog was
a dog.

In the darkness, knowing that the barkless
dog would be watching his every move from its
kennel near the house, Old Mwanza would walk
into the garden, his nostrils distending as he
savored the fresh smell of the vegetables. He
would close his eyes and try to think of the object
of all his love, past and present. He would see the
image of his wife. He would think of his wife
and the garden, the garden and his wife, his wife
and the garden, until the two would blend into
one individual unity. He would return to his bed,
his disturbed soul somehow satiated.

His daughter came the following Saturday
afternoon. Old Mwanza was ecstatic. She brought
him a cooked chicken swimming in curry soup.
As she warmed it on his primus stove in the little
kitchen, he cradled the boy in his lap. His daughter was a short, chubby woman who had the
cheeks and watery smile of her mother. She

smiled often, a sexy smile, which had drawn him, mothlike, to her mother. She was a healthy woman and he hoped fervently that her husband, a young man who worked for the government, was her equal. There was love between father and daughter.

Old Mwanza held the boy in his arm and watched with tenderness as his daughter prepared the chicken. She worked with the same effortless dexterity that he had loved in his wife. When she had cooked the *nshima,* they sat down to eat, talking quietly with familiar laughter and smiles, about their lives and about the boys.

"Jeremiah was at our house yesterday."

The daughter spoke with an imperceptible shake of her head, a nascent choke in her voice.

"What is it this time?" Old Mwanza squeaked with accustomed fright.

"He said you should not go on working. He says Mr. Parker is an evil man. He says things are going to be different soon. He says you fought for nothing in Malaya, now you are growing vegetables for nothing. He says you should be ashamed of yourself."

"This is an old story. An old story. He is young. How is Obadiah? He is older. He understands how these things are. Have you seen him recently?"

"No, Father, I have not seen him recently. He lives in Chibolya. You know what type of people live there. Criminals and prostitutes."

"Is he a criminal too? He was always very quiet. How does he feel? Mr. Parker says I am nearly sixty years old now. I cannot return to the village. I would not survive. My people have forgotten me. I have forgotten them too."

Father and daughter were silent. Old Mwanza enjoyed the chicken with much licking of the fingers. He wished they could leave some of it for the next day. He would hold a small party and invite the South African nanny. It could be the catalyst.

"Father, you know that something terrible is going to happen. Not to you. Something terrible is going to happen in the country. In the townships, they are talking wildly."

"Of what, my dear child?"

"Of things. Obadiah and Jeremiah, they may be different. But they say you should go to the village. They are always talking wildly."

"Of what?"

"Of the white people."

"What of the white people?"

The woman placed the plates softly into a dish of water. Her face was impassive, her voice steady and her demeanor unhurried. Only the wet smile was missing.

"They say they are evil. They say we should get rid of the evil."

Old Mwanza laughed nervously, trying to put derision to the laughter. His daughter turned abruptly to look at him in exasperation. The expression touched her face briefly, like a passing shadow. She was still his daughter.

"This is what Obadiah and Jeremiah are saying? My own children. They are mad." He laughed again, reflectively. "No they are just little children. Just children. The white man is evil? Who gave us Light? Who gave us God? Obadiah, he was a prophet. He called upon doom on Edom and predicted triumph for Israel in the Judgment. Jeremiah. He was a prophet too. A great prophet who was imprisoned for warning of doom. Your mother chose those names. She also chose yours, Esther. She loved God, your mother. All these things, who brought them?"

The woman was silent, sitting cross-legged on the floor, one big breast's dark teat in the mouth of her sleeping infant.

In a sudden, querulous voice, Old Mwanza exploded. "I am not a village boy. My people have forgotten me. We are strangers. You understand?"

The woman looked at her baby, serenely sucking on the teat. She nodded noncommittally. Old Mwanza was perplexed. "You understand, don't you? You are the oldest. You understand."

"Yes," she said, not looking at him. Old Mwanza shook his head in uncomprehending despair.

"No, Father. They are just wild, Obadiah and Jeremiah. They are just wild. They are wild to talk of driving out the white people. Forget about them, Father."

She rose, her practiced arms transferring the baby from her lap to back in one swift, fluid movement. Her breast, the milk dripping slowly from it, hung in embarrassment from her bosom. Old Mwanza did not look at her, his gaze examining in dawning consternation the uneven floor of the little room. He was a man to whom the Truth had been dramatically exposed as something less than pure, something foul and filthy, something he now looked at with deepening suspicion and mounting revulsion.

They talked on about known innocents, about truths that could be perceived, fathomed and comprehended at one uncomplicated glance. She talked about her husband, the great job he was doing for the government. He talked briefly about his garden, about his wife, her mother, and soon they lapsed into an embarrassed, tense silence, as each remembered the tender moments with the departed woman. Old Mwanza shook his head, as if to acknowledge his senile failure to grasp the true meaning of the new life.

That evening, after his daughter had left, he strolled through his kingdom, speaking quietly to his subjects, questioning them about Life and its lost meaning. He had asked his daughter to prevail on the two boys to visit him the next weekend. He loved the garden. Mr. Parker's relevance was receding. Neither he nor his family cared much for it. It was the only thing that mattered now, not Mr. Parker, not his wife, not his children.

He stood still and closed his eyes. His two sons came into focus. They were there, two short, powerfully built, younger replicas of himself, with the chubby smile of their mother and the primitive physique of their father during his heyday. They were dark, with short kinky hair which never seemed to grow to its natural length. Hard to comb. They were two good, good-looking boys. They were unmarried.

He smiled. Probably still sowing their wild oats. He remembered his predilection for the company of girls, many girls, different girls. If his wife had not threatened him so earnestly, if he had not grown up so suddenly, he would still be as wild. They were good boys, considerate and loving. When he returned from the war and found his wife sick, they cared for her while he searched for a new niche in a changed society.

They hadn't berated him for his purposeless absence. They should have, he realized with new insight. It had been a waste of manhood. He did not fight for anything that he knew or understood. The people of Malaya were small, but they had not called him to help their jungle war. He had always done what the white man asked of him. Even in the garden? Not the garden. He loved the garden. He did what he and Nature wanted done. Not Mr. Parker. He hoped fervently that his children would understand.

"Mwanza? Wena kona lo skopo. Wena yazi lo Mazungu en kona skopo maningi."[7]

---

7. "Mwanza? You have brains. You know that the white people have a lot of brains."

Old Mwanza knew that the white people were more than just ordinarily clever. People who could invent the airplane had to be extra clever. He did not need reminding. He did not need reminders of their unhuman cleverness. Mr. Parker said he, Old Mwanza, was also clever. That was because he did not believe, as did those fools in the townships, that he had even an iota of the cleverness of the white man, that he could conceivably devise anything, ANYTHING at all, that could rival anything that the white man had already created. The knowledge that he was clever because of his recognition of the white man's superior cleverness warmed him.

They were walking in the garden. Most of their conversations, most of their intimate exchanges, took place here. It was their common denominator. In the garden, Mwanza thought he was king. Mr. Parker did not, could not know it, but Old Mwanza watched his every move, lest he stepped on the vegetables. Old Mwanza did not know how he would react if he had.

Mr. Parker talked on in kitchen kaffir, reminding Old Mwanza that those stupid agitators in the townships were going to be punished most severely. It was explained that the authorities were preparing for the rascals. They had guns which spat smoke and some which spat real bullets. Did not Old Mwanza remember those guns? Hadn't he used such guns in the war in Malaya, when he fought for justice and freedom? Oh, yes,

Old Mwanza remembered them. Yes, didn't that mean that they would kill some of the Africans?

Of course, it did, but didn't Old Mwanza realize that if the authorities did not kill the agitators, they (the agitators) would kill innocent white people and perhaps innocent Africans, good Africans as well, such as Old Mwanza himself? Oh, was that the problem. The assurance gave him a real sense of security. Yes, people like Old Mwanza and himself, Mr. Parker, had to protect themselves (with the aid of the authorities) against the agitators who were nightly preparing to kill them.

In his bed that night, Old Mwanza trembled in indescribable terror. It hurt his atrophying limbs to know that death—his, Mr. Parker's or his children's—was in the air, that it could visit any of them now. People who walked innocently during the day, even the cook and the nanny, were plotting to kill, or had someone else plotting to kill them. There was a war on. It was nothing like the terrible business in Malaya, but it was there.

The next morning, Old Mwanza sought out the cook. They rarely spoke, the cook believing that his status precluded any obligation to speak politely to the gardener and the nanny. He was a thin, mustachioed young man who kept himself scrupulously clean, in a strange narcissistic way. The smell of an anti-B.O. soap floated above him like an invisible halo. He took a bath two times a day, forcing his naturally slovenly wife to do the same.

The kitchen window was high above the ground. Old Mwanza walked slowly from his garden and stood some distance from the window, speaking loudly and looking up at the cook, who was busy rinsing something in the sink.

"What do you make of all this wild talk in the townships?"

"What wild talk, old one?" he asked crossly.

"About what they are going to do to the white people, like Mr. Parker and his family?"

"Oh, that." The Oracle in him, flattered, opened up with haughty condescension. "It is much stupid talk. It is these people, who think they are educated. They want to chase away the white people. I laugh at them. No, I spit on them."

"So you think they are wild too?"

"Of course, they are wild." He leaned toward the window and spoke in a conspiratorial tone. "Can you imagine anyone being cleverer than the white man, than Mr. Parker?"

"I am happy that you think it is all wild talk."

"It is wild talk. You know, it is the hyenas, making all that noise when they cannot fight." They laughed. Old Mwanza walked back to his kingdom, his crooked step firm and confident.

"You are my children. I have always taught you the right way to behave. I want to teach you again today."

The two boys, casting furtive glances at the door, listened. Their eyes were impatient, darting

from the door to the old man, from the uneven
floor to the corrugated iron roof and back to
the old man. Old Mwanza spoke with paternal
authority and the assurance of one who is conscious of the infallibility of his advance. He sat
in the one chair in the room and they sat cross-
legged on the floor. They had arrived after he
had retired. He had not heard their footsteps
or any sound. He had not even heard the gate
opening and wondered how they could come
into the yard without alerting the deadly, silent
basenji. They could only have been allowed in
by Mr. Parker himself. After all, they were his
children.

"This foolishness must stop. I told your sister. It is impossible for me to return home. I am
too old. There is nothing for me there. Mr. Parker
is not an evil man. All white people are not evil.
What do you know about evil?"

Obadiah spoke. He was only slightly taller
than his brother, though they appeared to be iden-
tical twins. They were dressed in uniformly
threadbare nondescript clothes and the odor of
stale sweat filled the room.

"Father, if Mr. Parker were not here, what
would you do?" he asked nonchalantly, already
preparing his follow-up question.

"Well . . . I . . . would . . . what do you
mean, if Mr. Parker were not here?"

"What he means is, if we are able to arrange
for Mr. Parker's removal, would you go home,

even to confront strangers?" Jeremiah spoke with the same sangfroid.

Old Mwanza laughed, his spirit buoyed by Mr. Parker's assurances.

"I have heard the wild talk in the townships. It is like hyenas. Just loud talk. Your people think you are cleverer than the white people? Ha ha ha ha! You wait. They are preparing to deal with you. They have guns that spit smoke and fire."

"We know all about that, Father. We are also prepared. The point is, would you like us to remove Mr. Parker so that you can go home?"

"Now listen. Go back to the townships and talk to your sister. She knows these things. More than you do. She will advise you. Stop all the nonsense."

"Father," Obadiah said as they stood up languidly, their eyes still searching the room, catlike, "she is with us. Her husband is helping us. She told us to urge you to leave. She said she could not say so to you herself."

Old Mwanza wept when they had gone. Again, he saw his Truth being soiled, abused, dirtied and muddied. He walked silently into his garden, enveloped in a stygian[8] darkness of uncertainty. He spoke to the vegetables, and discovered with shame that no one, not his daughter, his sons, not his vegetables, listened to him anymore. In the far-off distance, he heard raucous, derisive laughter. He walked back to his house, his aching

---

8. **stygian** (stij′ē ən, stij′ən): dark and gloomy, derived from the river Styx of Greek mythology.

shoulders hunched, his head bowed, his mouth slack. People who appeared vaguely familiar seemed to be laughing at him.

In the night, he heard little that he could later associate with the bloody violence to which he was to be introduced. It was three days after his sons' visit, Old Mwanza could not reconcile himself to the truth, which was that his Truth had been mutilated and trampled underfoot by creepy, crawling monsters who said they were his progeny and bore no resemblance to him. He gazed for long minutes at Mr. Parker, even as he spoke while they strolled leisurely in his garden. He had forgotten his tragic toothlessness. Mr. Parker was a pitiable man. All the truth that Old Mwanza had gleaned from him, which Old Mwanza had embraced as universal truth, was being challenged. Old Mwanza tried to cling to his belief in Mr. Parker's invincibility.

Indeed, until the very last moment, until that apocalyptic moment, when his eyes saw what had to be seen, he still retained a residual faith in the power of Mr. Parker, in his cleverness and the cleverness of his race.

Absently, Old Mwanza wondered once more how the boys had neutralized the great basenji. He had felt the sleep creeping slowly upon him, like a thief for he had not wanted to sleep, being possessed of a presentiment once more.

They came to the door of his house, called him out in whispers and shepherded him to the main house respectfully, two sons taking their doubting father to a scene that would furnish incontrovertible testimony of their maturity.

The three children and Mrs. Parker were tied with pieces of torn bedsheets. They were tied so tightly that a uniform dull and deadly purpleness was spreading slowly up to their faces, as the flow of blood appeared to be slowing down. They were all on the huge four-poster double bed with the white eiderdown. They stared with long-gazed eyes at Mr. Parker who was on the carpet. Old Mwanza saw Mr. Parker's head split neatly in half, the short, sharp-bladed ax up to its hilt in the crown of his head. Mr. Parker was in his white tennis shorts. He was on his back and stared with blank, terrified, unbelieving eyes at the ceiling.

Old Mwanza looked from the inert body to his sons. He screamed a meaningless scream. He was screaming incoherently at his sons. Then he started to scream his wife's name. There was terror, disbelief and supplication in the voice. It was the mendicant wail of a recalcitrant child, begging its mother for forgiveness.

"You will return home now?" Jeremiah did not boast. He spoke with emotion.

"No! No! No! What about the garden? What about the garden? Will you give me a garden?"

He rushed at them, his fingers talons, tearing at their faces, wanting to obliterate their existence, as he had brought it into being.

They grabbed him easily and led him out of the house.

As they approached the gate, the old man's meager belongings fashioned into a crude bundle on the shoulders of Obadiah, powerful searchlights lit up the house and the whole yard. The basenji stood victoriously in front of the lights. They heard the familiar, commandingly insolent voice of a white police officer: *"Wena, funa ifa? Kabanga wena kumbuka tina dhlala kupela? Tina kona lo makulu gun. Makulu steleki."*[9]

There was a white man in pajamas whom Old Mwanza recognized as the man who lived at the next house. His eyes returned to the barkless dog, which Mrs. Parker had said was incredibly intelligent.

His two sons released him and retreated into the darkness behind them. He heard the roar of the powerful guns. He hit the ground as they had taught him in Malaya. He thought of the garden.

He wondered if the white police officer would shoot a man who spoke to vegetables in the dead of night.

■   ■   ■

---

9. "You want to die? Perhaps you think we are just playing? We have very big guns. Very big."

Chinua Achebe

(1930 –   )

Acclaim for Chinua Achebe's writing began almost immediately after the publication of his first novel, *Things Fall Apart,* in 1958. Dissatisfied with the representations of Africa and Africans produced by Western authors, Achebe sought to articulate within a novel structure a more authentic African voice. Achebe's use of the dialect and expressive forms of traditional oral culture, chiefly folk tales and proverbs, profoundly influenced later African writers. Some became identified as the "School of Achebe." Achebe has also played a significant role as a "social novelist," whose writing articulates and advocates the political causes to which he has been committed.

Born November 16, 1930, Chinua Achebe grew up negotiating two cultures. His extended family were members of Nigeria's populous Ibo ethnic group, but Achebe's father Isaiah converted to Christianity as a young man. Both traditional and Christian perspectives influenced Achebe's youth. As a young child he spoke Ibo, and he learned English beginning at age eight. Achebe's familiarity with diverse traditions, beliefs, and languages would later become an elemental feature of his literary approach.

Achebe entered University College at Ibadan on a medical scholarship, which he forfeited after switching to literature as the focus of his studies. After graduation, Achebe worked for the Nigerian

Broadcasting Service. Achebe has taught literature at the University of Nigeria, and he has held faculty positions at a number of American institutions including the University of Massachusetts, the University of Connecticut, City College of New York, and Bard College.

In addition to *Things Fall Apart,* Achebe has written four other novels—*No Longer at Ease* (1960), *Arrow of God* (1964), *A Man of the People* (1966), and *Anthills of the Savannah* (1987). Achebe has also produced work in several other literary genres. His publications include several short story and essay collections, poetry, and children's fiction. Achebe served as a founding editor of Heinemann's important African Writers Series.

Recognized as perhaps the most influential African writer of the century, Chinua Achebe has received numerous prizes and awards for his work. *Things Fall Apart* received the Margaret Wrong Memorial Prize. Achebe was awarded the Nigerian National Trophy for Literature for his novel *No Longer at Ease.* Considered by many Achebe's finest novel, *Arrow of God* received the *New Statesman's* Jock Campbell Award. *Anthills of the Savannah* became a Booker Prize finalist. Achebe holds several dozen honorary doctorates from colleges and universities throughout the world.

His convictions regarding the social purposes of art have involved Achebe in Nigerian politics. When the Ibo people of northern Nigeria attempted to form a separate Biafran nation in 1966, Achebe joined the cause. He served as spokesperson for the government of Biafra during the ensuing four-year civil war. In 1983, Achebe was elected Deputy National President of the People's Redemption Party.

Achebe married Christie Okolie, a professor, in 1961. The couple has four children, sons Ikechukwu and Chidi, and daughters Chinelo and Nwando. A 1990 automobile accident in Lagos, Nigeria, broke Achebe's spine. Confined now to a wheelchair, he still continues to write, teach, and maintain an active calendar of public appearances.

■ ■ ■